T0123463

SNOOKIE AND BERNIE ARE SWEETHEARTS

AN ANATOMY OF A MARRIAGE

SNOOKIE AND BERNIE BROWN

Inspiring Voices®

A Service of **Guideposts**

Inspiring Voices books may be ordered through booksellers or by contacting:

Inspiring Voices
1663 Liberty Drive
Bloomington, IN 47403
www.inspiringvoices.com
1-(866) 697-5313

ISBN: 978-1-4624-0684-5 (sc)
ISBN: 978-1-4624-0683-8 (e)

Library of Congress Control Number: 2013913058

Printed in the United States of America.

Inspiring Voices rev. date: 7/19/2013

This book is dedicated to our family:
those who raised us—our parents and their generation;
those who grew up with us—our
siblings and our generation;
those who came after us—our children
and their generation; and
those who hold the future—our grandchildren!

TABLE OF CONTENTS

FOREWORD

(From our children)

It is my feeling that children can only come to truly appreciate their parents after they have left home to start their own lives. My parents taught me core values that are ingrained in me today. My work ethic comes from my dad. I do not remember him ever missing work, and he gave it his all while there; he was highly respected as a CEO. He said that to be the best leader, you need to surround yourself with people who are strong where you are weak. An awareness of others comes from my mom. She included us in her social service activities from Faith-In-Action to helping at the Youth Museum to practically adopting two of her needy students. My frugal ways come from both, who demonstrated how to save money by making wise choices. They make an incredible pair, yielding higher results in their life together than either could have produced alone.

As Grammy and Pappy, they are wonderful grandparents, blessing each of our kids with unique and special gifts. But, they also give of their time to make things, sing and play the piano, bake and go fishing with them. Grammy calls my seventeen year old daughter just to talk, sends her letters of encouragement, care packages, and sometimes cash for no reason at all.

In recent years I've been blessed and privileged to get to know them not only as parents but as real people with joys and disappointments, strengths and weaknesses, just like those in the rest of the world. You will want to read this book by my special parents, two of my best friends!

-Jenny Brown Bailey (the first born)

★★★★★★★★★★

As I read my parent's story, I learned a few things that I didn't already know. I was a part of many of the experiences so could remember those, but at the time I couldn't see how God was working in their lives. It is interesting to look back and see how their faith and trust not only guided them but also how these virtues were instilled in us, their children.

I recall on one occasion, Mom and I were driving up to Lake Junaluska, NC for me to interview for a summer job. She made the comment that she might have made some mistakes along the way as she was raising me, but wanted me to know that she had done her best with what she knew at the time. I think I said something like, "That's ok, Mom," but what impressed me most was that she cared so much about me.

My dad was and continues to be an important mentor to me. Professionally, I chose a similar career (as a healthcare executive), and he has provided invaluable advice to me as my career has advanced. Even more importantly, he constantly demonstrates a caring, consistent and calm demeanor and spirit as a husband, father and friend.

I, too, am now a husband and a father, and my goal is to follow my parents' example with my own family. They continue to be role models for not only us but many others in their wide circle of family and friends. The most important lesson that I learned from them was that God loves me and they do, too.

Read this little book. It will make you laugh and cry, but best of all, it will make you think. And, as a result, you may gain a better understanding of what marriage should be all about.

-Jeff Brown (the favorite son)

★★★★★★★★★

When my parents celebrated their fiftieth anniversary, I had a friend call to say congratulations. I was kind of surprised she was congratulating me, but she went on to say that not many people have parents who stay together that long. I realized that I had probably taken for granted just how blessed I am to have parents who have been married for over fifty years. Their marriage has been a constant that all of us can depend on, even now as adults.

Looking back over my childhood, I think about our home being free from conflict. I know that we kids did our share of fussing, but my parents didn't fight. Sometimes I've thought, maybe that's not healthy – did they just repress their anger? But now I see. They did have some conflict here and there, but instead of holding onto it and making the disagreement drag on, they settled it quickly. The one time I witnessed my dad raising his voice to my mom, he walked out of the room and returned in about two minutes to give her a big hug and say he was sorry. I didn't even have time to get out of the way. I've found in my own marriage that I will say I'm sorry even if I wasn't at fault, because I don't want to be at odds with my husband. It doesn't matter who's right – if I win and he loses, we both lose. It's because we're on the same team. That's what I learned from my parents.

This book is special to me because it's about my family; it's our story. However, I think you will enjoy it, too. There aren't very many rock solid marriages out there, so I think we need to look closely at the ones that are. There is much we can learn from them. I hope that my husband and I can have a marriage that's worth reading about one day, too.

–Amanda Brown McLean (the baby)

INTRODUCTION

There was a country song written in the early 1900s that became popular once again when we were growing up. The first line was "Frankie and Johnny were sweethearts."[1] It was a sad story, as country songs often are, about a couple who began their relationship with a commitment "to be true to each other, true as the stars above." Johnny was Frankie's man, and "he wouldn't do her wrong." Well, you guessed it. He eventually did do her wrong, and she responded by doing him in! The last verse begins with "Now this story ain't got no moral, this story ain't got no end."

In contrast, *Snookie and Bernie Are Sweethearts* is a story about a couple in love who began life together with just such a commitment and are still true to each other more than fifty years later. Despite some challenges, stresses, and individual frailties, ours is a successful, fulfilling, exciting, and fun relationship. We believe without a doubt that there is a moral to our story, one that is contained in the wonderful state of matrimony long ago instituted by the God who created us.

We share these pages mainly for the benefit of our family—our children, grandchildren, and those yet to come—but are delighted if others have an interest in and can benefit from its offerings. When you reach your mature years, your memory can become foggy, and your recollections may get a bit distorted or even exaggerated (the latter is Bernie's forte). However, this is our best attempt to tell it like it is as we offer to you our testimony of love and commitment to each other. It may not be the racy type of love story sold in the romance section of your local bookstore, but it is heartfelt and pure.

Though this is our story, we will at times contribute separately, and in an attempt to give structure to the process, we will follow the pattern set in Bernie's recent book, *Purpose in the Fourth Quarter*, perhaps making this a type of sequel. In that book, his premise is that the game of life can be divided into four quarters with a break in the middle, similar to the game of football. Our life as a couple seems to fit comfortably within this template.

We feel the need to point out that we grew up in a time when marriage, family, and faith were three of the most sacred and important aspects of life as we knew it. Our parents who raised us were happily married and instilled principles of unconditional love and commitment within us. We realize that in parts of society today much has changed. The statistics of the number of children born out of wedlock are staggering, and many are not brought up by their own parents. Some are in poverty-stricken or abusive situations without good role models. These and other factors have resulted in many kids searching for the love of a family unit in all the wrong places. Therefore, we acknowledge that the challenges and obstacles are much greater today.

After reading our recollections, some might say, "That was just a fairy tale," or, "It was boring with not enough excitement and drama," and even, "They lived in another time." To all of these and any other reactions, we simply respond, "This is our story. It isn't boring to us but is rather an ongoing adventure, and in our minds, the principles of love and commitment never change."

Many of you also have interesting and insightful stories to tell, and we encourage you to do so! The exercise of putting our thoughts and memories down in writing has in itself been a time of reflection and has brought an even deeper commitment to and appreciation for one another. Most of all, it is our hope and prayer that this modest effort on our part will mean something to others seeking a Christ-centered relationship, and that it will honor Him, the One who created us and brought us together.

Chapter 1

THE GAME OF LIFE

> Everyone who competes in the games goes
> into strict training. They do it to get a crown
> that will not last; but we do it to get a crown
> that will last forever.
>
> —1 Corinthians 9:25

Purpose in the Fourth Quarter: Finishing the Game of Life Victoriously, Bernie's book, was published in late 2012. It compares the game of life with the game of football, which has four quarters with a break in the middle called halftime. In the book, the purpose or focus of each quarter as well as the overall purpose of life is explored. For those of you who have not read it, we will try to share a few of the pertinent messages it contains. Hopefully, these will be helpful in understanding why we think that this same template can also be applied when exploring the institution of marriage, its progression, its challenges and joys, as well as its purpose.

Over the years, the life cycle we humans experience has been portrayed in many forms. It has been compared to a race, a journey, even a battle, and it also has been likened to the seasons of the year. Bernie's book compares it to a game, specifically football. Irrespective of the choice of analogies, life is a progression that leads somewhere, and at its core, there is purpose.

In a football game, each quarter has its unique characteristics and focus, but in the end, the goal never changes. Likewise, in life, even though each quarter has a distinct purpose, there is still an overall purpose that guides us to victorious living.

Is it accurate, fair, or even appropriate to call life a game? What is a game? Dictionaries have some interesting definitions: sport, fun, amusement, contest, a field of gainful activity. Bernie contends that "life is a game, the most complex, difficult, and challenging with the potential of being the most rewarding, satisfying, and wonderful one played on the face of this earth." However, like every other game, there are competitive forces at work, and there are winners and losers. So for players in the game, the question becomes "What do you need to do to be victorious?"

One could look at life's progression from many angles, but Bernie believes that it can fall logically into four evolving periods with a break in the middle. It could be equally divided into quarters based on the average life span of an individual, but we all know that each person is unique, so the actual time required to complete each quarter will vary. The same types of clock-stopping events that occur in the sport of football can also happen in life, e.g., timeouts, incomplete passes, penalties, injuries, out of bounds, first downs, lightning strikes, and commercials. We could easily translate any of these into real-life experiences. It is amazing how many similar events can interrupt the movement of the clock in these two games. Yet there are also differences. For example, the game of football is played in a few hours in the afternoon or evening; the other takes a lifetime and beyond. Unfortunately, some are not given an entire life span to complete the game. But even in those cases, a life can still have purpose and be victorious.

Bernie's book concludes that a primary focus can be identified in each quarter, but at the same time, an overall purpose exists the entire time that we are on life's playing field. For your reference, here is a look at each quarter's focus and the overall purpose of life that the book reveals:

The First Quarter	Learning
The Second Quarter	Earning
Halftime	Midlife
The Third Quarter	Discerning
The Fourth Quarter	Yearning

★★★★★★★★★★

The purpose of life is to love God, your neighbor, and yourself and to receive and respond to God's love and call.[2]

After giving this much thought, we are amazed at the similarities between our individual games of life and our evolving life together as husband and wife. Could there be a connection here? We believe so and will share with you our experiences in each quarter as we have played out our game of life together.

Chapter 2

THE INSTITUTION OF MARRIAGE

> Which is an honorable estate instituted by
> God and signifying unto us the mystical
> union that exists between Christ and His
> Church.
>
> —*Ritual, The Methodist Church*[3]

Have you noticed that the actual process of getting
married these days is a big deal? Unless you eloped,
your wedding was a monumental event! Not even the
smallest of weddings takes place without much thought
and preparation on the part of the couple and the
extended families involved. Yet once the glory of that
special time begins to fade into everyday living, many
couples have found that they have made no preparations
at all for building a marriage and establishing a Christ-
centered home. Even those who are on the right track
are contending with a success-driven society that almost

seems to put marriage and family at the bottom of the list. The divorce statistics in our country are living proof that something is very wrong. In fact, this is a crisis situation for the time-honored, God-ordained institution of marriage, and Christians are not immune. It is surprising to note that the divorce rate among Christians is fairly comparable to the national average of about 50 percent. How's that for letting air out of some of our balloons?

So what is the institution of marriage all about anyway? Dictionaries define *institution* as something set up or established; founded or begun. *Marriage* is the act or ceremony of wedlock, joining together a man and a woman. Putting those together, the institution of marriage can be defined as the establishment of a joint venture called wedlock between two people, a husband and a wife. God's definition can be found in the Bible in Ephesians 5:31, which says basically that "a man will leave his father and mother and be united to his wife, and the two will become one flesh." (Bernie likes that wording best.)

The process of getting married involves procuring a marriage license and having a commitment time attended by witnesses and led by a pastor or person in authority that includes a recitation of vows of some type and a pronouncement that the couple is now man and wife. The specifics can vary, but nonetheless, all this binds a husband and wife together in a marriage covenant.

This is what we promised on our "big deal" of a day: "I, Bernie, take thee, Snookie, to be my wife, to have and to hold from this day forward, for better, for worse, for richer, for poorer, in sickness and in health, to love and to cherish, until death do us part, and forsaking all others, I pledge thee my faith." Snookie repeated the same vows. Then we gave each other rings with this response: "In token and pledge of the vows between us made, with this ring I thee wed; in the name of the Father, and of the Son, and of the Holy Spirit. Amen." That pretty much covers anything on the commitment path ahead without an ounce of wiggle room. We took it seriously then, and after fifty years, we still mean it!

In our eyes, this is what marriage *is*:

- A God-ordained covenant
- A contract between a man and a woman
- A joining together of two families
- A vehicle for procreation, providing the great joy of parenthood and, one day, grandparenthood
- A friendship requiring patience, understanding, and forgiveness
- A love like no other!
- A relationship that cannot flourish without the giving of 100 percent on each side

Also in our eyes, this is what marriage is *not*:

- The loss of individuality
- A place for self-centeredness
- Being dominated or dictated to by a mate
- To be entered into lightly or until something better comes along

- A battleground
- For sissies
- Perfect

And both lists can go on and on.

There are a couple of main things that we feel deserve more scrutiny in this chapter about the basic aspects of marriage. First, we have heard the whole issue of submission debated long and hard in many different arenas throughout our years together. This has never become an issue for us because we determined our individual roles early in our relationship. We know what the Bible says in Ephesians about the woman being submissive to the man and have even seen it taken out of context and misinterpreted constantly by those who hear what they want to hear. But for us it's like when Bernie was learning to dance. It didn't come easy for him, though he is musical in many ways. Then to top it all off, he found out that the guy has to lead! Once he got into the swing of it, though, he realized that it wasn't about him leading; it was all about the star, the gal, he was showing off! Snookie is a fabulous dancer. Marriage requires something on the part of each participant and then having the two of them work together to produce the final product, a beautiful dance.

We feel that ours is a Christian marriage ordained and blessed by God, whom we serve. Therefore, our goal is not only to live our lives as a united twosome, but to include Jesus Christ as the third partner in our covenant relationship. Let us tell you why we believe that this is so important.

Electricity has become a necessity in almost every aspect of modern life; we once saw an illustration using an electrical cord that has three wires. The current is delivered and returned through the black (hot) and the white (neutral) wires; the third wire, the green (ground) one, is for safety. In the event of frayed and broken wires, the ground wire lowers the risk of shock and even electrocution. Every marriage needs to be grounded by a third wire. We are only human. We are frail and flawed, but God is perfect and divine. He brings not only safety but life itself into this sacred relationship. We must always remember that He is the one who instituted this wonderful and honorable estate called marriage.

As our story unfolds, you will hear us from time to time refer to the term "Christ-centered marriage." We have come to realize that the center of our individual lives as well as our life as a couple is very small. It might be compared to the bull's-eye on a target or the hub of a wheel. What this means to us is that there is only space for one individual there. We can neither put ourselves nor our spouses there. For this to work, Christ, whom we both know and love, must occupy the center. *A Christ-centered marriage crowds out self-centeredness.* His presence does not detract from our love for and commitment to each other but, to the contrary, enhances both.

Chapter 3

FIRST QUARTER: AWAKENING LOVE

> God created human beings ... He created
> them male and female.
>
> —Genesis 1:27, *The Message*[4]

Beginning our story during the first quarter of life
obviously requires that we contribute separately when
exploring those years prior to the time we met. We sense
the importance of sharing this part of each of our lives
because of the effect it had on how we were developing
as individuals and how we feel we were being prepared
to one day become a couple.

Snookie's Turn

When I think of where I was born, I am always reminded
of the saying, "I wasn't born in the South, but I got
here as fast as I could!" Nothing against Kansas, my
birthplace, but I consider myself a Southerner through

and through. Actually, my daddy was stationed in Salina, Kansas, prior to leaving for Europe during WWII. My parents shared an apartment with another couple, and they were the ones who gave me the nickname that has stuck with me to this day. Mother endowed me with her complete name, Annette Bradford Rigdon, but I have never been anything but Snookie to those who know me. For all who aren't familiar with its origin, my nickname is a derivative of Baby Snooks, the main character in a 1940s radio program devoted to teaching children to mind their manners. It was acted out by the actress Fanny Brice when she was in her later years.

I grew up in the South Georgia town of Tifton right in the midst of both my parents' families. My life was centered on school and social activities, piano lessons, church functions, and on the prospect of one day becoming a majorette in the Tifton High School marching band. This lofty goal was obtained earlier than I even hoped for when I made it after trying out with the junior high band during my eighth-grade year. I then marched my way through high school, playing the flute during concert season.

My mother's parents lived around the corner in the next block, where I spent lots of time, especially when my grandfather was out of town on business. Granny didn't like being alone, so I slept right in the bed with her. To this day, I cannot smell Mentholatum without thinking of her and how she thought it warded off any possible cold. My daddy's mother, Grandma Rigdon, lived across the street from us. I didn't know my

Granddaddy Rigdon very well since he was an outcast as far as the family was concerned. He basically ran off with his secretary, which was frowned upon in those days. Grandma Rigdon was a fantastic musician who struggled to maintain her dignity despite having to play the piano at the Baptist church services with her ex-husband and his second wife in attendance.

The only time I lived any place else was during the couple of years my daddy went back into active duty in the army. As luck would have it, he was stationed not so far away at Fort Benning, right outside of Columbus, Georgia. So much for getting to see the world outside my hometown! We did meet people from all over, though. President Eisenhower's son and his family lived nearby, and we were fascinated with the men in the Secret Service who guarded them. I came home to Tifton with a Yankee accent that was difficult to shake, so I had to practice talking Southern to keep my classmates from laughing at me.

When I was in the eighth grade, Daddy was involved in a near-fatal automobile accident during one of his trips about the state selling life insurance. It was first announced on the radio that he had been killed, and my grandmother heard it. She came immediately to tell Mother, but we children never knew about it until later because soon after, someone came to say that he had been badly injured instead. I was by then the oldest of four children, two boys and two girls, with the youngest being a baby. Needless to say, life changed drastically for us, and I felt the keen responsibility to help out. And as if that were not enough, just as Daddy was recovering from his brain injury, Mother developed a serious case of hepatitis. I remember feeling that nothing was ever going to be all right again; my carefree, small-town existence was severely threatened. Family, friends, and the First Methodist Church, where we were members, came to our rescue.

The church was an important part of my life growing up. Methodist Youth Fellowship (MYF) with all its activities, church camp at Epworth by the Sea, fellowship suppers, Sunday school, and revivals were just what we did, and I loved it all. One of my best friends was the preacher's daughter, and with her I explored every inch of that church facility, even climbed up into the steeple! I have a fear of heights to this day and wonder if that's where it began. I do know that my position as Sunday school accompanist gave me the desire to be punctual! We only had one bathroom in our house, and it was quite a feat to get everyone to the church on time. Of course, the singing came first at Sunday school, and they had to wait on me to get there. As for revivals, I was always moved to answer "the call" at the end of the final service. Mother said she kept waiting for me to announce that I was going to Africa as a missionary when I grew up. I guess God was working in my life in ways that wouldn't show up until much later.

In reality, I have to say that anything of eternal value was quite far from my mind as a teenager. I was focused on parties, going to the movies, having friends spend the night, dancing at the local youth center, going to the swimming pool in summer, and having a boyfriend, which I always had. I thought I was in love with The One many times until I went off to college and found out what love really meant.

During my senior year of high school, I began to think about what I wanted to do next. I knew going to college was the best plan but had no idea where I wanted to go or if I even wanted to study for a career. Having a husband and children one day sounded like career enough to me. My daddy's whole family went to the University of Georgia, so I applied there and even considered trying out for the majorette squad. It seemed a bit large to me, though, so I also sent my application to Valdosta State College (now Valdosta State University). A visit to the latter convinced me that the smaller school was the way to go. Besides, tuition there was a better fit with my family's financial situation after all the troubles my parents had experienced earlier in my life. After a couple of years in college, I learned, much to my surprise, that my renegade grandfather helped in that regard.

Upon graduation from Tifton High, I took a month-long trip out West with my family. Picture this: Six people, suitcases for all, and camping equipment (including a camp stove, pillows, blankets, cots, sleeping bags, etc.) all piled into and on top of one station wagon with no air-conditioning. On the up side, we saw wonderful places in our great country that we had only read about until that point: Disneyland and Yellowstone National Park, Utah and its Mormon Tabernacle Choir, and Las Vegas with all the lights were among them. On the down side, there was just no getting away from siblings, and it was a struggle to get along in those close quarters for hours on end. Perhaps it was a foretaste of dormitory life and one day motherhood for me. Side note: We camped all the way out to California, even slept in barracks while Daddy did his Army Reserve camp duty. However, we stayed in motels all the way home. Even my adventurous parents had had enough!

My arrival on campus at VSC was a home run as far as I was concerned. I had a great roommate with whom I pledged the Alpha Delta Pi sorority, and immediately, we were thrown into sisterhood, fraternity parties, etc. The college fellowship group at First Methodist sent cars to pick us up for church activities, dorm life was like a continuous slumber party, and, oh yes, I went to classes too. It was heaven for me to be on my own. I dated a lot of the college guys but still sort of had a boyfriend back home—until he came to visit one weekend. It was then that I realized I had moved on. I was growing up!

Toward the end of the first quarter, I began to notice a really nice guy named Bernie Brown. He was the brother of my friend Suzanne and was often around when I visited her home. He was older and didn't seem to see me as anyone other than his sister's classmate. Besides, he had been on a few dates with one of my sorority sisters, and I didn't plan to get in the middle of that! In time, though, her boyfriend reentered the picture and Bernie was back on the available list. I couldn't believe it when he called to ask me to a birthday party for one of our friends. To me, he was the good-looking big man on campus (BMOC), president of his fraternity, Who's Who in everything, and glee club soloist, and I was a lowly freshman. However, I went to the party with him and right away found out one thing he couldn't do well—dance! And alas, knowing how to dance was one of my requirements for The One! Since everything else was lining up very quickly, I decided that I'd better begin teaching him the jitterbug (now called "swing") on our very first date.

Now Bernie's Turn

My full name is Bernard Loam Brown Jr. My dad had always disliked his middle name but for some reason chose to pass it on to me anyway. Loam is a form of dirt, so I understood his feeling. Therefore, I'm glad that my parents just called me Bernie. I was born in the 1930s. If my mom had waited just thirty-four more days, I would have been born in the 1940s and not seem so old.

Dad was a Methodist preacher so that made me a PK (preacher's kid), which in itself carries a perceived connotation. In my day, PKs, particularly boys, either turned out really good or very bad; I still haven't figured out my fate. Back then our denomination regularly transferred its ministers every four to five years, so I never lived long enough in one place to put down roots. Dad was in the South Georgia Conference, so the five places we lived while I was still at home were in the

Deep South below what is termed down there as the "gnat line."

I had one potentially serious health issue when I was nine. I had a series of seizures, and the doctors suspected epilepsy. I was taken to Emory University Hospital in Atlanta to visit one of the few neurologists in the state at that time. In those days, we did not have the benefit of CT scans and MRI procedures. I had an EEG that was considered the state of the art technology at the time. I was placed on medication that I took at every meal for the next year and was told to not play too hard or get too tired. Almost a year later, I returned for another visit, and all the tests seemed to indicate that the problem had been alleviated. But when I stopped taking the pills, the seizures returned. I had become addicted to the medication. It took another year to be weaned off the pills, and all has been fine since. From that experience, I learned the effects that an addiction can have on one's life and health.

I never considered us poor; we certainly weren't poor in the things that mattered. I learned later that my dad's top annual salary was just twelve thousand dollars, and of course, we were provided with a place to live and a whole lot of groceries from farmers and friends. During my early years, Mom sewed and made most of our clothes. I remember hoping to one day have a store-bought shirt with a label. Mom handled my request by removing one of the labels from dad's worn-out Arrow shirt and sewed it into one of mine. An aunt and uncle gave me my first authentic one, which I wore on special occasions.

Until I reached high school, we lived in small towns in rural areas. Then we moved to Savannah where I attended Savannah High, one of the largest high schools in our state at the time. What a contrast! I was truly a country boy coming to the big city.

Infatuation with the automobile had not yet hit, so our family always had just one car. It was either black or white because the preacher always led funeral processions to the cemetery, and any other color would look mercenary and be too flashy. Then, when I was a junior in high school, I got my first car. Dad and I entered into a joint venture; we each paid half of the $150 with the understanding that Mom could use it for her activities from time to time. It was a blue 1950 Plymouth two-door coupe. It needed some work, so with the help of "Uncle" John Deason who owned a service station, I rebuilt the engine and installed a glass-pack muffler. I put fender skirts on the back and spinner hub caps on the front wheels. My mom made velvet covers for the sun visors (one was blue and the other was pink), and I used some left-over red carpet from the church sanctuary to cover the floor that was partially rusted out. It was always interesting to see Mom drive up to the grocery store in one of the loudest and flashiest cars in town. My friends dubbed my beautiful mode of transportation "the blue seducer." What a misnomer for someone like me.

In high school and the first year in the local junior college, I began to notice how attractive many members of the opposite sex were, but I had only a few dates and never a regular girlfriend. I had only sisters, so I guess I primarily thought of girls as siblings. My attitude was somewhat influenced by my best friend's mother who told him, "If you kiss a girl, she could get pregnant, and I will kill you if you get a girl pregnant." I took this more to heart than he did because he always had a steady girlfriend. To be honest, my greatest interest was the outdoors, camping, hunting, and fishing, which distracted from any lofty social and academic pursuits. (To illustrate this, my picture in my senior yearbook appeared in only two places—with my class and as a student assistant in the office.)

I did have one out-of-character passion: I wanted to learn to sing. The youth choir director in our church had told me to just move my mouth without sound during anthems, as evidently many discordant and off-pitch tones were coming out. However, she had to let me sing since my dad was the preacher. Not to be outdone, I paid for private voice lessons from my salary that I made working at the local grocery store. Interestingly, though, I had never participated in any school music activities.

I auditioned and was selected to be the male soloist at my high school graduation. Most in attendance at the large stadium were surprised and even shocked to hear a booming baritone rendition of the Lord's Prayer coming from an unknown like me. I believe that this one experience was God's way of telling me that I had worth and something to offer. Therefore, that was the beginning of a definite change of direction in my life. My school had not been my place of social development, but in retrospect, I now see that my church filled that need through Sunday school, youth fellowship, choirs, and camps. And I had the same wonderful pastor and his wife throughout all those years—my dad and mom. The presence of God was truly in my mind. After all, He was my dad's boss!

Then Dad was appointed District Superintendent for the Valdosta District. Valdosta was a nice-sized town with a four-year college, so I transferred there to begin my sophomore year. I was rushed by and pledged one of the largest fraternities, sang in the glee club and ensemble, played on the tennis team, and became very involved in campus activities. Looking back, that was when I truly crossed the threshold into manhood. You would call me a late bloomer. I became president of my fraternity, a soloist in the glee club, an officer in student government and Circle K Club, doubles champion and all-conference in tennis, was selected for Who's Who in American Colleges and Universities, and voted Best All-Around student in the senior college.

During this time, my dating habits also took a 180-degree turn. In the summers when I returned to work at the grocery store in Savannah, I probably dated more than a dozen different girls, and during my sophomore and junior years, I had steady girlfriends on three different occasions. Entering my senior year, I eyed a very attractive freshman girl who had a long-standing boyfriend back home. My venture into this relationship proved to be futile and soon fizzled.

A surprise birthday celebration for a friend of my sister was planned, and we were all invited and expected to have a date. At the time, I was single and trying to decide whom to invite. Running through my list of prospects from the past led nowhere, and I was about to gracefully decline the invitation. Then my mom, who was never without suggestions or the desire to help, asked, "Why don't you invite that cute girl from Tifton who is your sister's friend. Snookie Rigdon?"

What a special night that turned out to be. I even learned how to really dance! Until the day she died, Mom claimed credit for the relationship that grew and flourished from that very first date. In an effort to keep her humble, I later contended that God used her for this purpose, to which she conceded. At any rate, that was the beginning. Snookie and Bernie became sweethearts!

From the Two of Us

It is hard to coauthor personal memoirs, but we will do our best to make this as understandable as possible. For example, what pronouns do we use? At times, we catch ourselves saying "I" when we should say "we," and often we need to use "he," "she," or "they." So bear with us if this becomes confusing at times.

In most cases, a great first date doesn't end without setting another. Both of us have a love for music (Snookie is an accomplished accompanist, and Bernie sings), and we discovered that we both enjoy the same type of music, mainly Broadway. So we agreed to meet at a practice room in the music department and have a sort of a jam session. We played and sang a lot of things, but what we remember most is "Some Enchanted Evening" from *South Pacific* that ends with "Once you have found her, never let her go ..." Incidentally, the practice room was soundproof, so we will say no more!

At this point, Bernie had two quarters remaining before graduation and Snookie was completing her freshman year. He had already applied and been accepted to the Program in Health Care Administration at George Washington University in Washington, DC, and would begin the following fall semester. So this became an important factor as our relationship grew. I (Bernie) hate to admit this, but one of the early attractions to the field of health care administration came from two hospital administrator acquaintances who told me their annual salaries were twelve and thirteen thousand dollars, more than I ever dreamed of making. In fact, my goal was to have a salary of thirteen thousand dollars a year before I retired.

It may not have been love at first sight, but it was love after the first couple of dates. The balance of the school year was spent getting to know each other better. In those days, college rules were much different. For example, there were curfews, dress codes, and a lot of behavioral rules and regulations, mainly directed at coeds. Our grandkids would die laughing at some of them. So during the week, our routine was to go to the library in the evening and then by the student center for chocolate milk with ice and barbequed potato chips before returning to the dorm. On the weekend, we usually had a date on Friday and/or Saturday and church activities on Sunday; all of these were less restrictive. The local drive-in theater was one of our favorite places that allowed us more time to get to know each other better. Though there was a high-octane attraction between us, we chose to draw a line in regard to what was called then as "going all the way" before we were married. We have never regretted that decision.

We made a couple of trips over to Tifton. The first was to attend a dance, and the other was to meet all the family, including Snookie's grandparents. I have two experiences that stick in my mind. Brad, Snookie's youngest brother who was about six at the time, asked me in front of the entire family, "Are you going to sleep with Snookie tonight?" This was an innocent question because her girlfriends usually slept with her when they visited, but it didn't help my situation as a suitor. And Snookie's grandfather, whom they called "Goo Guy," asked me quite seriously what my intentions were concerning his oldest granddaughter. I assured him that they were honorable. I guess I passed my initiation.

In March, we were "pinned" (Bernie gave Snookie his fraternity pin to wear), which was a pre-engagement step that openly expressed the deepening of our relationship. We had another little experience that certainly shows our age. We exchanged framed copies of the first colored photos we ever had taken of ourselves. Interestingly, this was before color photography, so the actual colors were brushed or painted on manually. Wow, how things have changed!

It became obvious that a serious romance was brewing, so our two families saw the need to get to know each other better. Snookie's parents were a bit concerned, with justification, since she was only eighteen at the time. It's only about an hour's drive from Tifton to Valdosta, so Bernie's mom and dad invited them over for dinner one evening. It was a fun evening with our excusing ourselves to let our parents have their time together. To be honest, we were a bit uncomfortable and wanted to be alone anyway. We returned just before the party ended and noticed that Snookie's folks were leaving with a Chihuahua puppy from the Brown's dog's recent litter. That puppy, Skip, lived for almost fifteen years and was a constant reminder of the merging of not only two individual's lives but also two families.

The balance of the school year flew by and climaxed with Bernie's graduation. Snookie stayed at Valdosta State for the summer quarter so we could be together. Since neither of us had a summer job, we, along with Bernie's sister Suzanne, devised a way to make a little money to assist with college expenses. We traveled almost every weekend to present concerts at churches throughout South Georgia. Love offerings were collected and divided between the three of us.

It was a sad day when Bernie left for graduate school at GW. We knew that it would be Thanksgiving before we would see each other again. In retrospect, we now realize that this was much more difficult on Snookie than Bernie. She was back in her familiar place at school, unable to participate in all the social activities that required a date. Her typical weekend was spent serving as monitor as all the girls in her dorm came and went on their dates. Bernie's situation was much different. Washington was the farthest he had ever been from home, and the demands in the graduate program were overwhelming. He was the youngest in his class, so the challenges and rigid schedule became his main focus. He was constantly in a survival mode.

We exchanged letters almost daily. Because of the mail service back then, we would often receive several letters the same day that required checking the postmark so they would be read in order. At least once a month, we set up a telephone call that had to be coordinated with the pay phones in Snookie's dorm hall and in Bernie's rooming house. A quarter was deposited about every three to four minutes. This was not an easy time. Absence may make the heart grow fonder, but it also fosters deep loneliness. No doubt we both grew individually and collectively from this separation that lasted nine months.

Thanksgiving was coming. Because the holiday period was short, arrangements were made for Snookie to travel to meet Bernie at his Aunt Martha's home in North Carolina. Her mother and siblings would leave her there while they went on to Tennessee to visit relatives and would return to pick her up on the way home. Bernie planned to ride the bus down to Hendersonville for the long weekend. Unbeknownst to Snookie, the following letter had been sent to her mother and father earlier.

> Dear Mr. and Mrs. Rigdon,
> I am looking forward to being with Snookie at Thanksgiving in North Carolina. I wish I were back home so I could come over and ask you this personally. I want to marry your daughter and desire to have your permission and blessing. I plan to give her an engagement ring when we are together. I love her deeply and will assure you that I will support and take care of her in every way. I know that she is young, but she is mature and wise. I hope and pray that she will accept my proposal and make me the happiest person in the world.
> Thank you for making me feel welcomed and a part of your family.
>
> Love, Bernie

Incidentally, a response came back shortly with their permission and blessing.

As we approached our destination, my (Snookie's) mother asked if I could get out the directions to Martha and Tex's house and make sure we were on the right road going into Hendersonville. The blank, panicked expression on my face told her that we might be in trouble. In rushing to get home from college so we could leave for NC, I hadn't even thought to bring the letter with all the information we would need. The next question was "Well, what is their last name so we can call them?" I didn't know. "Is Tex his real name?" I didn't know. "Is there anything that you *do* know about them?" was the final question as we crossed the city limit line. About the only thing I knew was that Bernie's grandmother was staying with them. "What is her name?" Oh, I knew that too. Her name was "Grandma."

In recalling this incident, Mother said that she had never been so mad at me. However, she has always been resourceful and self-sufficient, so she found and stopped at the Chamber of Commerce welcome center. "We have a problem. We are looking for a couple named Martha and Tex, don't know their last name, and her mother, Grandma, is staying with them." Now don't tell me that God is not involved in our lives. The Welcome Center lady answered without hesitation, "You're talking about Frank 'Tex' and Martha Watson. Her mother is with them. They are my neighbors, and here is how you get to their house." A miracle had occurred! However, whether I was as mature and wise as Bernie thought is up for debate.

Bernie arrived late in the afternoon. When he stepped off the bus, there was no kiss or even a hug. He was green from motion sickness after riding in the back of the Greyhound bus through the narrow, winding roads of the Smoky Mountains. It took a couple of hours before his nausea subsided and normal color was restored. What a way to start one of the most important weekends of his life!

The next day after some rest, Tex loaned us his car and suggested a couple of popular sites in the area. One of these was Chimney Rock, a famous attraction at one of the higher elevations. I (Bernie) was careful to drive slowly; I didn't want to have another bout with carsickness.

It was a cold but beautiful clear day, and the attraction was not very crowded. After a brief exploration of the surroundings, we stood by a guardrail. Quite unlike the fanfare involved in today's marriage proposals, I simply reached in my pocket, took out the ring, kneeled down, and asked Snookie to marry me. She knew it was going to happen sometime that weekend but still hugged me with excitement and said, "Yes!" By now, I was well enough to kiss.

After we prayed and asked God's blessing, we talked a little about the wedding. I agreed that Snookie and her mother should handle all the planning because I would arrive home only a few days before the big event. We stayed another day in North Carolina, and then I boarded the bus for the return trip, this time doped up with Dramamine to prevent the nausea of the earlier mountain trip. It was hard to leave, but I knew that it was only a month until Christmas when we would be together again.

Bernie rode the Silver Bullet to and from the railroad stations in Washington, DC, and Nahunta, Georgia, twice more during the last semester. An administrative residency was required as part of the health care administration program. He was assigned to the University of Alabama Medical Center in Birmingham and would begin work two weeks after our wedding. Everything was shaping up!

However, a few weeks before the end of the school year and after all the wedding plans were finalized, I (Snookie) began to take a serious look at what I was about to do. I had just turned nineteen, was only a sophomore in the middle of my much-anticipated college experience, had never really been on my own financially, and was about to move far away from my family. I knew that I loved Bernie, but I hadn't seen him since Christmas and had hardly been able to even talk to him, so I just wasn't sure about the timing. My mother was, as we say in South Georgia, fit to be tied when I announced all this to her. But she saw my confusion and suggested that I come home and talk with my pastor.

He did the best he could, but to no avail. I dreaded most having to tell Bernie how I felt right in the middle of his tough master's program. But when we talked, he told me to not change a thing until he came home for spring break. I did as he said, and when I walked into his arms in front of my dorm the day he returned, I knew everything was going to be okay. God knew all about the timing, and it was right.

The events surrounding our wedding on June 17, 1962 at the First Methodist Church in Tifton turned out to be much more dramatic than anyone dreamed. Bernie's sister Suzanne met her guy, Robert Taylor, had a whirlwind courtship, and decided to get married the week before we did. Bernie's dad, who performed both ceremonies, was reassigned to a new pastorate scheduled to begin the week after our wedding, plus they had a two-year-old daughter, Mary Kay! Despite all this, our wedding turned out to be a wonderful family event. Suzanne got back from her honeymoon in time to sing "O Perfect Love;" our brothers, sisters, and friends were participants in our wedding; and the church was filled with well-wishers.

We can't leave this day without covering the "going away" and the honeymoon. We changed into our going-away clothes after the reception and headed through a shower of rice to our borrowed car to leave for St. Simons Island. To our amazement, every inch of Bernie's dad's car was covered with messages and pictures, and each wheel was carefully placed into the halves of Georgia-grown watermelons!

We had very little money for a honeymoon, so we were dependent upon the benevolence of our relatives who came through in a big way. Snookie's aunt and uncle, who lived on St. Simons Island, offered the use of their home while they were away on vacation. They even stocked the refrigerator for us, which became a topic that would be discussed for many years.

At the reception, we had missed out on the punch and cake while in the receiving line greeting our guests and we were hungry. So, we decided to make a ham sandwich right after we arrived at the house. Someone (we both deny it) picked up the family-sized glass jar of mayonnaise, but the top wasn't on tightly. The jar slipped to the floor, spraying its contents all over the kitchen with most of it landing between the slats of the louvered doors of the pantry. Needless to say, we spent our first few hours as man and wife on our knees cleaning up mayo before it dried. So much for a romantic beginning to our wedding night! On top of that, Bernie's fraternity sweetly sent us flowers with the instructions that they be delivered as early as possible the next morning. They must have paid some florist a lot of money to get up before dawn to do that!

(An important side note: After the mayo episode and we were ready for bed, we got down on our knees and prayed an elementary but most sincere prayer for God's blessing on our marriage. We were scared, as neither of us had experienced such intimacy before, and we knew that God needed to be in it with us. And He always has been!)

Our big night out was financed in a most surprising way. We had rationed our money carefully so we would have enough to eat at the Red Barn, a really nice restaurant on the island where Snookie's uncle Joe had made reservations. Also, her pastor had unexpectedly returned the wedding fee we had given him, so we knew we had that to fall back on. After our meal, Bernie asked for the check and was told that it was already covered! What we didn't know was that Uncle Joe was close friends with the owner and had paid for our meal in advance.

The next day, we headed back to Tifton to pack up and move to Birmingham, Alabama, where we would begin our married life together. We finished our first quarter as we left our original homes, declared our independence from our parents, and established a new family unit. When the preacher closed our wedding ceremony with "It is my pleasure to introduce you to Mr. and Mrs. Bernie Brown," we were twenty-two and nineteen years old.

"I love you!"

"I love you!"

Lessons Learned in the First Quarter

1. Each one of us is unique. Even though we may have some things in common, many factors influence who we are as individuals.
2. An inherent need exists in each of us to be a part of something. We do not want to be alone in this life.
3. Some good things can come from bad experiences.
4. Doubts are acceptable and need to be faced honestly.
5. God is working in our lives during the first quarter even though we may not notice it as much as we will later in life.
6. Physical attraction often ignites a relationship but open, honest, and genuine commitment helps it endure.
7. The first quarter of life in the context of marriage may be classified as *awakening love*.

Chapter 4

SECOND QUARTER: GROWING LOVE

> For this reason a man will leave his father
> and mother and be united to his wife, and
> they will become one flesh.
>
> —Genesis 2:23

We arrived in Birmingham pulling a trailer behind our much-used Renault Dauphine and settled into our one-bedroom unit in the Park Lane Apartments. This was in the Mountain Brook area, one of the highest per capita income communities in the country, at least until we moved in and brought the average down! We would live there for two years.

Bernie began his administrative residency at the University of Alabama Medical Center under the preceptorship of Dr. Matthew McNulty, one of the top health care executives in the country. Snookie enrolled as a junior at Howard College (now Samford University) to complete her degree in sociology.

Looking back, that was one of the most invigorating and fulfilling times in our lives. We had very little money and, aside from wedding presents, few possessions. The net income from the residency stipend was $150.00 per month and half of this went to rent. That left us about seventy dollars to cover all our other expenses (food, utilities, gas, etc.). But we were so much in love that we didn't know how poor we were. Interestingly, our tithe to our church didn't seem so much, just five dollars a week.

As the new kids on the block in Bernie's organization and obviously (to everyone else) needy, we were constantly given tickets to events, ballgames, concerts, and the like. Joe Namath was the quarterback at the University of Alabama, so we got to see him play several times. On one occasion when no one else could go, we hosted Lord and Lady Baird, a delightful dignitary couple from England during a formal visit for a special event. They had never ridden in the backseat of such a small automobile, but they seemed to love it! We were allowed to be a part of many other university and medical center activities and reveled in it. An interesting side-note: Controversial Alabama Governor George Wallace was then the chair of the medical center board by virtue of his office.

On one occasion, we were asked to attend the annual University of Alabama president's reception, representing one of the senior executives who didn't want to drive over to Tuscaloosa. We arrived at the mansion in our faithful Renault that was promptly valeted and parked among all the Cadillacs, Lincolns, limos, etc., symbolic of our lowly status in those circles. But it didn't matter to us, as we were blissfully enjoying it all. While wandering around in this beautiful place, I (Bernie) accidently but literally bumped into the only person there who looked familiar. When I apologized and introduced myself, the man responded, "Glad to meet you. I'm Paul Bryant." I had just personally met and shook hands with Coach Bear Bryant!

On campus at the college, I (Snookie) had an entrance appointment with the dean of women. This nice but quite formidable lady looked across her desk and informed me that I was much too young to be married, and that I was welcome there but would be missing much the school had to offer socially. I went away with a smug little smile, knowing just how wrong she was about me.

Our daily routine began with my taking Bernie into the city, dropping him at the hospital, and going back over the mountain to classes. Our little blue car made the trip fine but was not quite so cooperative when I got ready to leave. First of all, I had to park on a hill to ensure a running start or I might be in trouble due to the serious need for a new battery. If the car wouldn't start and I was blocked between two cars, I had to get a piece of notebook paper, go to the back where the motor was housed, remove a certain hose to the carburetor, cover the hole with the paper, get out the crank, insert it into the engine, and give it a hard twist. Not too many cars had a crank! (You can tell by my explanation just how knowledgeable I am about the workings of a car.) Besides that, shifting gears was relatively new to me. Often in heavy traffic and on hills I would roll backward, nearly touching the car behind me, so I wouldn't risk a huge bump if I had a problem getting into the next gear.

When I picked up Bernie after his day, we shared the different aspects of our lives all the way home. Though we were both extremely busy, it was a time of growing friendship for us as husband and wife.

In my classes, it was quite different from my VSC days. I was a student but not part of the college scene. Although I was the same age as my classmates, I was married and my life was at home with Bernie. Many of my classmates were far from settling down; one guy even asked me for a date! So I guarded my heart, kept myself out of uncomfortable situations, and sought the friendships of other students like me. Looking back, I know that God was with me, developing me into the kind of wife I wanted and needed to be.

Career Begins and Family Expands

As Bernie's residency and Snookie's college career came to a close, a "what now?" decision needed to be made. An offer to remain in Birmingham was on the table, but we chose to move to Gulfport, Mississippi, where Bernie accepted the position of assistant administrator at Memorial Hospital. The instant pregnancy test was not available back then, so unbeknownst to us, Snookie was expecting at the time.

About eight months after our move, our firstborn arrived on February 12th. She and Snookie remained in the hospital for several days. Two days following Jenny's birth, Snookie had a meltdown. Postpartum depression, or the third-day physical/emotional adjustment, was my (Bernie's) nonprofessional diagnosis, but I discovered this was rooted in something else. In a tearful voice, Snookie asked me, "Do you know what today is?" "I sure do," I said. "Jenny is three days old, and we are getting ready to go home." Wrong answer. "Today is VALENTINE'S DAY!" I forgot this special day in 1965 but never again in the forty-eight years since!

To say that becoming parents blew us away would be an understatement. We were mesmerized by this tiny girl who was so perfect in every way. She had the dark hair and hairline of her maternal granddaddy, the round face and pug nose of her mother, and the slender body of her dad. At her baptism, we dedicated her little life to the Lord and promised to raise her in the church and in the knowledge of her Heavenly Father. We also made another decision that we have never regretted. Our marriage would take the direction of teamwork. Bernie's work would be ours together, as well as the raising of our child and any others to come.

Life changed dramatically once we had the added responsibility of a child. We were no longer two but now a family of three. Nurturing our relationship became a challenge, as did attending hospital functions and getting together with friends. Since both sets of grandparents lived so far away, hiring babysitters became a necessity. It wasn't easy at first to leave our little girl, but it was another maturing phase for us as a couple and for Jenny as she learned to adapt to those who cared for her.

Our little Methodist church was a big part of our life and one of Jenny's biggest adjustments came in the church nursery. One Sunday, Bernie was singing in the choir and I was in the congregation when we heard an unmistakable cry that would not stop. We kept looking at each other, trying to decide who was closest and would cause the least disruption in the service. We rescued her that time but persevered, as we wanted her to feel at home in her church. Eventually, she looked forward to going to the nursery.

One of the responsibilities of my (Bernie's) job was to establish and oversee the human resources function for the organization. In this area, a primary duty was to counsel and assist employees with their careers and work challenges. One afternoon, a young lady about my age and probably the most attractive female in the entire organization made an appointment to see me. Almost immediately after she arrived, she began to share not only job related but also personal problems and became emotional. I guess she felt somewhat uncomfortable about that because she asked if we could close the door. Eunice, my assistant, who incidentally was about the age of my mom, was sitting at her desk in the next room, and I could see the frown on her face. I thought a minute and said, "I'd rather not because, as you know, we have an 'open door' policy that not only means everyone is welcome but also that nothing inappropriate is going on behind closed doors." That seemed to satisfy her, and Eunice smiled. I can't say that I never closed the door to my office, but I became ultrasensitive in my job as a leader and, more importantly, my role as a husband. In looking back on this early career experience, I can only conclude I was divinely guided.

After three years in Gulfport, Preacher's Kid Bernie felt it was moving time, so he began looking for another opportunity. We wanted to be closer to home, but it didn't work out exactly that way. An opening at the North Carolina Memorial Hospital in Chapel Hill, North Carolina, became available, and since it was in a university setting much like Birmingham, we felt a nudge to explore it. This started a spiral of events that landed us there but not in the home we planned to purchase.

Once we knew the job was secured, we made a weekend trip to buy a home. Our next-door neighbors were going to purchase our Gulfport house, so we knew just how much we had to spend. We selected a place, put money down, and returned home to pack. Just before we were about to leave, our agent called, letting us know that we needed to come up with five hundred dollars more in order to get the loan for the property. There we were, making $750 a month, stretched to the limit on what we could afford, a packed moving van in our driveway, and no place to send it! With heavy hearts, we drove to Bernie's parent's home in Dublin, Georgia, to figure out what to do next. As it turned out, Jenny stayed with her grandparents while we made the trip to Chapel Hill, picked out another house, and met the moving van at the Carolina Inn. They unloaded the very next day. God knew what we needed, and it wasn't that initial home, which would have stretched our budget to the max. He was teaching us good stewardship. We were in training and didn't even know it!

Great Sorrow and Return Home

My (Snookie's) parents came to visit during the summer while we were in Chapel Hill, and we noticed that my daddy seemed tired and had a constant cough. Mother said that they were planning to check that out when they got home. Little did we know that our world would soon be turned upside down. The diagnosis was lung cancer, and my outgoing, positive-thinking daddy would not live until his fifty-first birthday. This was the first time I had lost anyone that close to me, and it just didn't seem fair. It hurt so much. He would never know his first grandson; only our daughter Jenny had the benefit of feeling this granddaddy's love. This left an enormous space in my mother's life, of course. She became a widow at only forty-eight with one child in college and two still at home. She was an inspiration to me in the way she trusted the Lord to carry her through, and I've never forgotten her testimony to that fact.

We stayed in Chapel Hill just long enough for Bernie to gain more experience in a university hospital and get in some UNC basketball games at the old Carmichael Gym. I also had opportunity to teach some piano lessons and to discover more about what it means to be a supporting wife in Bernie's work endeavors. We had made that teamwork decision, and it became ever more obvious that God was honoring our commitment. I was pregnant again and gave birth to a little boy who would become a lifelong Carolina Blue fan. So proud to have a son, we named him Jeffrey Bernard!

We had not been in North Carolina for even two years when these homesick Georgians got a chance to go home. A job in Augusta at the University Hospital became the vehicle for this move. We tucked our baby boy into his infant seat on the floorboard of the front seat, stuck Jenny in the back with some books and toys, and headed south.

In Chapel Hill, although we had joined a church, we had never really found a church home in which to grow our faith, so we were anxious to do that back in Georgia. We visited around and landed smack in the middle of a warm congregation with an outgoing pastor and a good choir. We still have close friends to this day from that church. During that time, we went on a choir retreat up to Lake Junaluska, North Carolina, with two-year-old Jeffrey pointing out every Volkswagen along the way just so he could say that big word. As you will see, that wonderful trip turned out to be providential.

Three years in Augusta gave us time to experience the Masters Golf Tournament a couple of times. Bernie even played the course twice. The second year, we were about to head out to the course for the final afternoon of play when Jeffrey, who had just learned to walk, slipped in his bedroom and broke his leg. He had to be in a body cast for six weeks. During that time, we had an out-of-town meeting, so his grandparents agreed to babysit for both children. Troopers that they were, they hauled our heavily casted son around for several days. He had such a great attitude or it would have been much worse, and we developed muscles we didn't know we had. Plus Jenny, just old enough to help out, was at his beck and call. Our family was a unit; we were learning to depend on each other.

In addition to that meeting away from our children, Bernie and I sought other opportunities to spend quality time together. In the early stages of our marriage, Bernie had spent a good bit of what I considered to be family time with his friends on the tennis court. We talked it out and agreed that balance was a necessity, though we didn't always see eye to eye on exactly how that would work. First love so easily can get pushed into something resembling humdrum routine, and we didn't want that to happen to us. We wanted to keep that spark alive even in the midst of demanding jobs both away at the office and in our busy home. God showed us how at every turn.

The University Hospital in Augusta was in the midst of one of the largest building programs in the region. The old hospital was being totally updated to a state-of-the-art facility. This would prove to be a wonderful experience and of immeasurable value for the future.

There was some turmoil in the leadership ranks fueled by personality conflicts, different styles of leadership, personal values, and priorities. Looking back, some of the best and most important lessons were learned from this. Many times, it is more valuable to know what *not* to do as to know *what* to do. Certainly, all organizations have similar dynamics to some degree.

The Ultimate God Incidence

In late 1970, Bernie was contacted by an executive search firm and asked if he would be interested in a chief executive position at Kennestone Hospital in Marietta, Georgia, a large suburban medical center. He had never been beyond assistant administrator, and this was his first chance to be seriously considered for the top spot. At the time, he was only thirty years old. We talked it over and approached it as a learning opportunity; after all, he was surely too young and inexperienced.

After submitting all the appropriate information and reference checks, I (Bernie) learned that I was in the final six and then shortly afterward that I had made the top three, each of whom would be interviewed by the Board of Trustees. On a stormy afternoon, I had a rocky flight from Augusta to the old Atlanta airport for my meeting in the early evening. I had a rental car reserved but soon would be faced with a crisis. Motion sickness, my nemesis, was already manifesting itself, and then I learned that my driver's license had expired, and therefore, I couldn't rent the car.

Time was wasting, so my only alternative was to catch a taxi. I had very little cash, and the cab drivers would accept neither a credit card nor a check. A C&S Bank branch was in the airport but was closed for the day. I happened to notice that although the door was locked, there was someone still inside. I knocked and finally attracted the attention of the gentleman there. I told him I was from Augusta and implied that Mr. Bennett Brown (the bank's CEO from Augusta) and I were related, so he was kind enough to cash a check. I arrived about fifteen minutes before the scheduled interview, having prayed all the way during one of the most exciting and harrowing rides of my life. I was not praying for wisdom and guidance but instead that I wouldn't throw up in the meeting!

Though the details of the meeting are a little blurry to me now, the one thing I do remember is being brutally honest. I shared my shortcomings along with what I believed were my strengths and expressed concern that the organization had a reputation for high turnover in the position for which I was applying. A major building program was needed badly, and much discussion centered on my experience in that area. After the interview, the search consultant drove me back to the airport and indicated that the decision would be made that night. He would call those not selected, and Mr. Little, the board chair, would call and make an offer to the one they had chosen.

When I arrived home very late, Snookie was waiting and wanting to know every detail. My ultimate analysis was that there was no way I would be selected. I went to work the next morning and pretty much got into the swing of my old job, as we had agreed I had done the interview as a learning experience. Later, my assistant buzzed in to tell me Mr. Mura (the search executive) was on the phone for me, thus indicating that I had not been selected. "Mr. Little will call the one chosen" echoed in my mind. But when I answered the phone, Mr. Mura said, "Mr. Little would like to talk with you." I was offered the job with a starting salary of twenty-six thousand dollars, exactly twice what my early goal was to make by the end of my career. This was not coincidence; it was Providence (or what Snookie calls "God incidence").

Early on, it was obvious that the responsibilities and demands in this new role were much different from my previous jobs. Even though I felt confident and prepared, I was younger than almost everyone on the hospital and medical staffs. In an effort to appear older, I grew a mustache. Thirty years later, I shaved it off in an effort to look younger! Recruiting key staff, developing and nurturing relationships in the institution and community, restructuring the organization, planning for a major expansion program, and changing the corporate culture were just a few of the early foci. There were meetings constantly—breakfast, lunch, dinner, and on weekends. Some days I would start work at 7:00 a.m. and return home after 10:00 p.m. During this period, Snookie led the effort to establish our new home, get the kids settled, volunteer in our church and community, as well as be the first lady of our new organization. Time, or more specifically the lack of it, was rapidly becoming an issue. What about our relationship and our team approach to which we had committed? All this was not easy, and although our commitment and love never wavered, it was obvious that we needed to find solutions to this escalating problem.

Remembering What's Important

About this time, we signed up for a marriage enrichment workshop that was held at our church. Two very special principles came out of this. First, we needed to be intentional about our own relationship and give it priority. This was my (Bernie's) problem primarily, as the job was taking precedent over my family. As a result, I began formally placing family time on my calendar and not allowing it to be usurped. I remember times when meetings or other potential conflicts arose. I would look at my calendar and indicate that I already had something important scheduled at that particular date/time. I was once asked by my board chairman if I could change my appointment to accommodate something else. When I told him that Snookie and I had planned to do something together and had made babysitting arrangements, he not only withdrew his request but congratulated me on keeping my priorities straight.

The second principle was simple: We needed to pray together regularly as husband and wife. We were doing this on an individual basis but only together for meals and during times of crisis. At that point in our lives, neither of us prayed often out loud, so this meant that we would share with each other what we were sharing with God. At first, it was a bit awkward, but as time went on, it became powerful. Over the years, it has evolved into a meaningful three-way conversation and growth in spiritual oneness.

About two years after arriving in Marietta, we received some wonderful news. We were going to have another addition to our family! We had thought four children would be nice, like the families in which we were raised, so were happily headed that way. Amanda Annette Brown arrived during a huge spring thunderstorm, but her personality was just the opposite. From a tiny girl, she was the most adaptable, peaceful child I (Snookie) ever knew. Perhaps it was because her sister and brother were so busy she had to adjust and go along to all sorts of activities. Or maybe she was just born that way. In any case, we felt so complete with this family of three children that we called her the baby, and that was it!

In time, my mother returned to her love of the arts, selling her paintings at shows, teaching and helping establish the local art association. She also started going out with a few men in Tifton, and I was truly happy for her to be ready to do that. My brother Brad had a close friend, Alan, whose father was also widowed, and Mother started seeing him on a regular basis. This led to a marriage that would last even longer than her first. Howard became the grandfather that many children would know. In this I also saw the Lord at work. God's provisions for Mother were ongoing.

Time management was not only an issue with Bernie. I came to discover that volunteer jobs can become every bit as consuming as paying jobs! I remember being in charge of the elementary school spring fair right on the heels of giving birth to my third child. I had accepted that role back before I knew I was pregnant, so I was on course to see it to completion. What was I thinking? It was a true lesson in balancing balls in the air, and I'm sorry to have to admit that I didn't get the message the first time. It was sort of like forgetting the labor in childbirth once the joy of having the child arrive safely took over. Those kinds of events were seasonal, only lasting so long, but then there was always another one waiting in the wings. I had to come to grips with the fact that I wasn't Super Mom or Super Wife and didn't have to prove to myself that I could be. My family needed me, and I could space out those opportunities until the children were older.

Our whole family was blessed to be a part of Marietta First United Methodist Church during those years of growth. The children were content there from the nursery on up; one of them even remarked that she felt good just driving into the parking lot. We attended youth camp every summer, which was not only great fun but was an unbelievable spiritual experience for parents and children alike. It was a heyday for this church that we loved so much. The youth choirs went on choir tour right after school let out for the summer each year,

SNOOKIE AND BERNIE ARE SWEETHEARTS

and we as choir parents were a part of that as well. We couldn't have asked for a better place to have our kids involved. Most importantly, all three accepted Christ as their Savior during that time!

Besides being the busy mom of three—we had a child in each of the three levels of city schools at one point—I was learning to be what my friends called the "first lady" of Kennestone Hospital. I had responsibilities in this new role that I had not experienced in Bernie's previous positions. Lots of head tables at lots of dinners where they always seemed to serve broccoli (not something I eat) with lots of people seemingly looking at us were in my schedule. Often there were important speakers for me to help feel welcome in our midst. I especially remember sitting by columnist Celestine Sibley, actor James Brolin, comedian Jerry Clower, First Lady Rosalynn Carter, and Chick-fil-A founder Truett Cathy among others. There were also dinners and open houses in my own home, entertaining board and staff members, doctors and their wives. I was stretched in my abilities to be an innovative hostess and to roll with the punches, some of which were not natural for me. I especially had a hard time dealing with the vulnerability of Bernie's position and the sometimes-critical words pointed his way. It was then that my fangs came out! However, looking back, I see that during those times I was learning to receive and show God's grace in uncomfortable situations. Bernie's and my relationship as a couple deepened because we were in it together—a real team.

Our children grew to appreciate their dad's field of work. We were privileged to travel not only to the summer hospital meetings for the Georgia Hospital Association but also to national conventions, visiting cities like Toronto, Montreal, Chicago, Houston, New Orleans, and several in California that they had only read about. These turned out to be priceless family times with other hospital families who became close friends. A memorable occasion involved all five of us dressed up and dining in a huge ballroom complete with mirrors on the ceiling. The kids were complaining about the fancy food, especially the cold black bean soup placed before them. Our son Jeff announced in a loud voice after looking up at the reflection in those mirrors, "Look, Mom. No one else is eating this stuff either!" Refinement was a constant work in progress.

Our parents still lived in South Georgia, so we got to visit both Tifton and St. Simons Island now and then. Spring break was spent each year at St. Simons with an extra child for each of ours in tow. The station wagon was piled high with people, luggage, and beach equipment. One of Amanda's best friends was Ashley, and though they loved each other dearly, they could only handle so much togetherness before that relationship was tested. So we established the "time apart" rule with each in a separate area until they could make up and happily start all over again. That type of situation became known in our family as "two dogs in a pen." Most dogs can exist side by side in harmony for a while, but then they start barking and snapping at each other. Feelings are out in the open, and once soothed, life goes on.

In raising our children, one of the things we learned was how important it was to *allow them to fail.* There is the temptation for parents to fix or to intervene at every turn to prevent adverse consequences for their children, and we were no exception. But if our kids don't experience failure while they are young, they won't be able to handle it when they are older. In this area, we were not perfect, but we tried, and as a result, we have watched them all face many challenges and even handle failure gracefully.

The Nest Begins to Empty

Our children began to leave the nest one by one as they graduated from Marietta High School. Jenny went for a weekend to visit Berry College in Rome, Georgia, and although she looked at a couple of others, that one seemed right to her. Thus began a four-year relationship with this special school that emphasized a well-rounded college experience, including a work program for its students. We missed her terribly both for herself and because the complexion of our little team of five was beginning to change. But we knew that our job as parents was, like the mother eagle that puts thorns in her nest, to not make the nest too cushy but rather to give our offspring wings to fly out on their own.

Jenny came home for Christmas after that first semester. While we were catching up, she collapsed into tears in my arms. I was surprised because I knew how much she was enjoying college life. But what I didn't realize was how much she missed her family and her home. Her wings were gaining strength, but her heart wasn't ready to let go. I assured her that independence didn't mean leaving it all behind; she still had a support system that would be there for her. It was an endorsement of all that Bernie and I had sought to provide for these children we loved so much. We had given them roots that were deep and binding.

Jeff became our only link to all that was happening at the high school, and that was tough. He even remarked one day that he would never be like his sisters, telling everything he knew. And he was true to his word. We had to depend on the neighborhood high school girls and his best friend, Scott, to keep us informed. Next, it was his turn to leave home, and he had only one school in mind, Georgia Southern University in Statesboro. He pledged Sigma Chi and loved the social life. By his sophomore year, though, he discovered that to go any further in his education, maybe even graduate school, his coursework had to take priority. And this paid off. Jeff subsequently earned both an MBA and a master's degree in healthcare administration from Georgia State University.

Amanda was our singer and musical theater enthusiast, so she was leaning that way as she looked at colleges. Her church youth choir director advised her that if she could go into any other career field to do it, but if her heart was leading her to music, it was a calling. In other words, the arts would not be monetarily profitable and jobs could be scarce. After much thought and prayer, she selected Samford University, her mother's alma mater, and proceeded to follow her heart. This gave us another college campus to visit as well as a chance to go back to Birmingham where we started our life together. We had come full circle.

Amanda got to share her love of music, particularly musical theater, with lots of folks. Besides being on stage in shows of her own, she spread this joy among the young people she taught and directed while on the staff of Marietta High School.

As the final chick left the nest, our second quarter ended. There would be a slight pause before we would move into the second half of our game. In retrospect, this period had been an endless series of opportunities, adventures, and challenges. But through it all, our love grew, and we were truly blessed.

"I love you!"

"I love you too!"

Lessons Learned in the Second Quarter

1. You are often better off with less.
2. A friendship between spouses that is continually growing is important.
3. You need to guard your heart and mind at all times.
4. Family should be given the highest priority.

5. Begin early to exercise good stewardship of time and resources.
6. Depend upon and complement each other; you are a team.
7. Learn not only what to do but also what *not* to do.
8. Pray together regularly.
9. It is important to allow your children to fail.
10. In the context of marriage, the second quarter of life is focused on *growing love.*

Chapter 5

MIDLIFE: CRISIS OR COMMITMENT

A fool finds pleasure in evil conduct, but a
man of understanding delights in wisdom.
—Proverbs 1:23

In Bernie's previous book, *Purpose in the Fourth Quarter*,
midlife in the game of life is compared to halftime in
a football game. It is the break in the middle of the
game that can be positive or negative. In the marriage
relationship, midlife can be a crisis for some while a
point of recommitment for others. We all know those
who have suffered through midlife crises. Midlife by its
very nature causes us to pause and evaluate where we
have come from and where we are going. It is the point
in time when, under normal circumstances, we have
lived about one half of our lives.

Our break occurred as our children left the nest,
and we were alone again in our big house with three

empty bedrooms. Interestingly, this probably had a more dramatic effect on Snookie because the nest over which she had presided was now empty while simultaneously Bernie's job was reaching its pinnacle.

Though we had made the decision for me to be a stay-at-home mom while our children were growing up, I had never regretted getting my college degree. This made me think back to when Jeffrey came home from school after a discussion about careers, saying, "Mom, Carol's mom is a nurse, and Bobby's is a teacher. What do you do?" I told him that for me raising him and his sisters, being involved in their activities as well as in mine, and being a supportive wife to his dad took all my energy and was one of the best careers I could imagine. It hadn't been easy to finish that college degree after marriage, but I was glad to have it and in time discovered that I had been using it all along, just in other ways.

I was proud of Snookie's adjustment as we paused to enter the second half of our lives. She by nature is outgoing, energetic, and proactive; therefore, to her, it was a matter of refocusing. Late in the second quarter before Amanda, our youngest, left for college, Snookie accepted a position as a paraprofessional assistant in a kindergarten class in the local school system. She did this first on a full-time basis and later in a job-share situation for several years. This proved to be a bridge into the second half for her and also a blessing for many children. Friendships from that experience still exist to this day.

Not so much in our lives but rather in those of some of our acquaintances, we have sensed an emptiness and even restlessness when the family unit protracts back to only two at home. No doubt the emphasis and focus on children for many years sometimes can erode the appreciation and intimacy that initially existed between the founding partners of the family. On the other hand, a renewed sense of freedom and flexibility is now available to the couple that can in time provide a rekindling of the closeness of the relationship.

Certainly, our children were as important to us as ever, but they just weren't present on a day-to-day basis. Interestingly, in a couple of instances, two of them returned home for economic reasons while attending graduate school and launching a new career. And we learned that things were different now; we had to recognize them as independent adults even though they were back again in their same beds. This was hard initially on both parties and required some discussion and ultimate agreement on how this new arrangement was to work. However, our change from constant to periodic encounters has led to even deeper and more meaningful relationships with them as adults. To this day, we light up each time we see our children, their spouses, and our grandchildren.

In my previous book, I noted that many midlife crises are the result of immaturity and the unwillingness to go on with your life. This may be caused by a first half too fraught with failure or too filled with success, leaving you with an unhealthy desire to stay put. Hence, there may be a hesitancy to move on and become a successful second-half team.

At halftime in a football game, the team retires to the locker room and analyzes the first half's performance in order to determine the strategy and focus for the second half. The coach leads the session with input from the players. How should this work in a marriage? Snookie and I took stock at this particular juncture, and it was obvious that our lives were changing in many ways. What had we learned that would be of value in our second half?

First of all, conflict does come. Wherever two or more are gathered together in a tight space, there is potential for the "two dogs in a pen" theory to manifest itself. The secret is to not let it fester, or as the Bible prompts, "Do not let the sun go down on your anger." Neither of us can stand the silent treatment or harsh words for very long, so we tend to get it out and move on.

Secondly, even though we were still young in our own minds, we couldn't help but begin to see that life wasn't going to go on forever. One of our fathers had died at age fifty, and the other began to have serious health problems in his early sixties. Shouldn't we be thinking about taking care of these bodies that God had given us? We began to take an even closer look at our diet and exercise. It hadn't been easy to modify these things to promote a healthy lifestyle and may never be. After all, we live in a society quite prone to not only equate lots of food with fellowship but also to sit down on the job, unlike our ancestors. We had been trying even when our children were still at home to make good health a priority, but we could do more.

I (Snookie) had begun to go to the YWCA when Amanda was a toddler and then later to Health Place at the hospital to participate in the aerobics classes that had become so popular. I even felt remiss when I couldn't get there. In fact, my friends (some known only by first name) and I were an accountability group through those sessions, keeping each other faithful in this quest to stay in shape. I was feeling pretty good about myself and decided that this was the way to do it; I would just sail into old age, healthy and active! But fast-forward to midlife and something called *menopause.* All women are familiar with the acronym PMS. Magnify this state of emotional upheaval many times, and there you have menopause. This can manifest itself in extreme hormonal swings, hot flashes, night sweats, etc. Though my symptoms were not as severe as some endure, it was still a challenging time. I saw and felt changes that made me a bit wistful for life before wrinkles, spider veins, and dry skin. My emotions were often on edge, and Bernie learned to duck when necessary! He was my knight in shining armor, though, as he encouraged and loved me through it all.

Thirdly, we had developed deep respect for each other as husband and wife and needed to continue seeking ways to show that. Both of us are the eldest in families of four siblings and like to be in charge. Yet it's obvious that both can't be. So we developed a divide-and-conquer approach. Bernie can't sew (only because he hasn't tried), and I don't use power tools (because I am scared of them). I make curtains, garments, and dust ruffles and hem and repair seams; Bernie builds, remodels, and repairs almost anything. We paint together, but I do the trim while he does the roller. I am also good at holding the flashlight or the other end of a long board when necessary.

So the question became "Where do we go from here?" Thank goodness we had the best coach of all time: a heavenly Father who had been coaching marriages since the beginning of time. In a nutshell, the issue was this: were we going to follow His game plan, or were we going to flounder without one or with an ill-conceived one of our own making? We chose the Coach's plan. To this point, we had evolved individually and collectively as a couple from *dependence* to *independence* to *interdependence*. We were as much in love as ever and chose to recommit ourselves to each other for our balance of the game.

"I love you more than rice pudding!"

"I love you more than caramel cake!"

Lessons Learned at Halftime

1. Midlife can be a vulnerable time that can result in crisis.
2. Midlife also can be a time of renewal and recommitment.
3. In any case, midlife is a time of reflection, reassessment, and redirection.

4. When children grow up, we, as their parents, need to set them free.

5. To this point in our lives, we have evolved from being dependent to being independent and then as marriage partners to being interdependent.

6. As never before, we need to heed the guidance from the Coach during this period that immediately precedes our entry into the second half.

Bernie with his parents –1941

Snookie with her parents – 1943

Bernie in high school – 1957

Snookie in high school – 1959

Our wedding – 1962

With our children – 1983
Jenny, Amanda, Jeff

With our grandchildren – 2012
Noah, Greta, Nathan, Jordan, Lindsey, Alexandria

Our new grandchildren
Amanda and Brittany Bailey

Our family
Snookie, Bernie, Greta, Lindsey, Susan,
Alexandria, Jeff, Noah, Brad, Jordan,
Amanda, Nathan, Jenny, Marc

Practicing hospitality

Chapter 6

THIRD QUARTER: MATURING LOVE

As for me and my house, we will serve the
Lord.

—Joshua 24:15

The beginning of our third quarter truly was a new
game for us. We had now completed our first quarter
(awakening love), our second quarter (growing love),
and during halftime (midlife), we had done some
assessment of our marriage to that point. The second
half of our game together would require not only a
change in direction but also a change in mind-set as
our children began lives of their own. There were
many role models for us, some who were handling the
third period with grace and meaning while others were
struggling for answers to the "what now?" question.
Their children had been the glue that held them
together.

At this point, we began to view life from a broader perspective. To some extent, it gave us more freedom, time, and opportunity to grow in areas that had been unintentionally neglected. Instead of wondering how we were going to get everything done, the new mindset was to focus on important ways we, as a couple, could make a difference. Our spiritual lives began to rise to a new level, and our own relationship expanded and deepened. Maybe our first half of life had taught us some valuable lessons that we could now apply even more effectively. Our love was moving into its maturing phase.

Heavy Hearts and New Roles

The third quarter began in a very traumatic way for me (Bernie). I will never forget the call from my dad's doctor saying that he had suffered a massive heart attack and was in critical condition. Eighteen years earlier, Dad had had a stroke. He had been a workaholic and didn't handle stress very well, which I believe contributed to its cause. The stroke had taken a physical and mental toll on him, and his quality of life had deteriorated over that extended period of time.

The next few weeks were a blur as we made trips back and forth from Marietta to St. Simons. Dad died at the age of eighty. It was especially tough for me as the oldest child and only son in my family. Dad and I had had a special relationship. When you go through times like this, your spouse can provide such wonderful and much-needed support. Snookie loved my dad and shared my loss. It's true intimacy to be able to cry together. After this, I set a goal to retire from my full-time position at age sixty-two (my dad's age when he suffered the stroke). In my mind, Dad's death also created a new role for me: I became the patriarch of the extended Brown family.

At this point, we had been married almost thirty-five years. In my eyes, Snookie had always looked and acted youthful, and now she was evolving into not only the cutest but also the most beautiful woman I had ever seen. I was seeing her more and more as God saw her. From the time when we first started dating, we found connection in holding hands, and three taps or squeezes delivered to each other said, "I love you." As we returned to a twosome once again, we felt that we were more in love than ever before. Still holding hands and tapping three times.

Bernie is saying some nice things about me, but then he always has. Any husband out there can learn from him. I have never doubted his feelings for me; in over fifty years, I have received only love and encouragement. He makes me feel like the belle of any ball, like I am the only one for him. I want to do my part to let him know I share that sentiment in return. In my estimation, there's hardly anything he can't do if he puts his mind to it. He is blessed with many talents and makes the most of them in any given situation. He always says, "Men can be the scum of the earth at times," referring to his theory that men lead in the causes of marital turmoil. I don't know about that, only that I got the exception to such a rule. He's the best!

Handling Finances

We should probably have included a discussion about money in every quarter because there is no doubt that this is an important subject in marriage. In surveys of married couples, we have learned that finances can be one of the most contentious and destructive issues in the relationship. Here is our take on this.

Neither of us was raised in an upper-income environment, so we have a typical middle-class spending mentality. Our favorite shopping places still include Belk, Walmart, T. J. Maxx, Target, outlet malls, etc. A bargain at a sale is something we both seek and pride ourselves in finding. Unfortunately, we do from time to time purchase the wrong item because the price was so right. We share this to say that we don't consider ourselves overly materialistic.

The one thing that we agreed on from the start was that we would tithe at least 10 percent of our gross income to the church. If we chose to give to other charities, that would be in addition to the tithe. We did this when we were making $150 per month and then when our income grew to six figures a year. This has resulted in some interesting experiences.

One year early in my career, we decided to pledge an extra four thousand dollars above the tithe to a church mission program. This was something that we had not planned, so it was sort of a faith promise. When the time came, we took the four thousand dollars out of our savings and made the contribution. The very next week at the hospital board meeting, my annual evaluation was conducted. The chairman met with me afterward, and in addition to my merit raise, I was given a forty thousand dollar salary adjustment because surveys indicated that my compensation was not comparable to other CEO's in similar positions. Please don't misunderstand the meaning of this God incidence. To us this was not a "prosperity gospel" event; the adjustment might have been made even if we had not made the extra contribution. Still, it served to remind us that God honors our faithfulness and that we can trust in His provision for us.

Another conscious decision that we made was to not change our lifestyle as our income grew. In so doing, we placed most of our salary increases, bonuses, investment income, etc. into our savings to be used for our children's education, emergencies, retirement, etc. We also believe in living as debt free as possible; the only outstanding debt we have incurred is a home mortgage that was paid off ten years early. We always planned toward having enough to pay cash for our automobiles, feeling that a car payment was a burden we wanted to avoid.

Being prudent and responsible is a lifestyle choice, and it has served us well. However, we realize that everyone is not in a position to handle things the way we have. We have been abundantly blessed from a financial standpoint. However, we continue to attempt to exercise good stewardship with the material assets that we have been given while constantly reminding ourselves that acquiring and owning "stuff" should not be life's main objectives.

The Pinnacle: Home and Job

You've heard the expression "God works in mysterious ways." As you have read, we tend to call those types of things "God incidences." Take the buying of our home where we now live, for example. We have friends who live on a lake, and they used to ask us to house-sit while they were out of town. They have a pool and a boat, so who could say no to that! The house across the lake from them was built by the developer of both the lake and the property surrounding it, and we had only seen it from the boat. One day, a friend of ours who knew how much we loved the area called to say that the house was going up for sale. We got in touch with the owner right away and, bringing Amanda along, went to see it.

As we entered the huge double front doors, he told us that the doors came from the old First Methodist Church (our church) when they tore it down after relocating and the slate on the floor in the den came from the roof of that same sanctuary. And it just got better. The wooden beams in the enormous living/dining room were from an old warehouse, and the siding in the first bedroom was salvaged from a rustic barn that stood on the property in the subdivision where we had lived for twenty years!

"This was meant to be our house," Amanda and I said over and over. Bernie was trying to hush us, not wanting the price go up. Long story narrowed down, we bought it over the weekend after the owner said he would take our current home as part of the deal. Not only that, the realtor involved decided to buy our home herself so it never even went on the market. We had a special dedication time with family and friends to bless our new home and pledged to use it as a ministry of hospitality. We have now lived for over twenty years here in Happy Valley!

Our third quarter would prove to be period of dynamic growth for my organization. Kennestone, the original hospital, would evolve from a single institution to a multi-hospital system, including a large physician group along with many ambulatory and other health-related services. It became one of the largest nonprofit community health systems in the country. The governing board, leadership, and staff were seasoned, and most had worked together for an extended time.

During the latter part of the second quarter through midlife and into the early years of the third quarter, I was approached by several other organizations about CEO positions. Although I felt complimented and, in a couple of instances, had conversations, I always concluded that I was where I was supposed to be. Mine had been a unique situation; there was constant growth and development. With the challenges and opportunities in the health care field coupled with a wonderful, supporting community, a career that normally would require several moves to advance allowed this move-prone professional to spend thirty years in one place. The third quarter would prove to be the climactic period for my career. We were truly blessed.

Just as I was proudly watching Bernie reach the pinnacle of his career and was involved with him in many aspects of that, our children began to find their mates. This meant participating in the wedding planning, with all three ceremonies at our church. It also prompted a decision for me. After several years of working at the elementary school, I realized that my responsibilities at home were building up once again. Working with kindergarteners had been a joy for me, but with the marriages of my grown-up children, I anticipated having little ones (grandchildren!) coming into my own family. So giving up my job was a natural progression for me.

An avocation that I truly didn't realize I desired came along about the time my paying job ended. It was seasonal, which fit into my schedule better and became a joyful challenge for me. Our church had many theater enthusiasts, so a group of them got together to form an outreach ministry. It was called "Jubilation" and designed to not only use the talents of our church members but also those in the community who wanted to audition for a summer musical. I love Broadway but was not blessed with the abilities to either sing or act. However, actors need costumes, and I can sew. Thus began my venture as a costumer.

My first assignment was to hem mountains of red-and-white checked tablecloths for the dinner theater production of *Cotton Patch Gospel*. This led to about twenty years of working with one of the best costumers around who encouraged me to stretch myself. I made it my mission to not only be authentic with the costumes but to make sure that those I dressed felt good about themselves in what they wore. Also, I was able to share many of those shows with our daughter Amanda, who got all the talent for being on stage, which I missed!

At probably the very peak of my (Bernie's) professional career, a conflict occurred that led to a public confrontation with the local newspaper. Being the organization's leader, I became the target. This is one of those most-feared situations for someone in a high-profile job like mine. Not only was I attacked professionally but also often personally. The advice from several of my best and wisest friends was "You can't win a public battle with someone who buys ink by the barrel!" The details are not important, but for almost a year, the local press constantly smeared me. In all this, my greatest lesson was that my dear wife was my staunchest ally. In addition to comforting, counseling, and defending me, she was truly my God-given fortress. At the end of the day, I looked forward more than ever being in my home with a loving, caring, and devoted wife who shared my load. In time, the situation calmed down and actually ended without residual damage. I learned many lessons from this experience, and through it all, Snookie's and my love grew even deeper and wider. Our little team rallied to meet the occasion.

Staying Young by Sharing

Another fulfilling opportunity fell into my (Snookie's) lap at that point in time. I had never thought about the term *mentoring* when I was busy doing my stint as a church youth volunteer. Shortly after our move to Marietta, we became counselors to middle school kids and then gradually moved up with our own kids to the high school group. This included Methodist Youth Fellowship, church youth camps and the small group gatherings following those weeks, church youth choir, and also many musical productions where I often did costuming with young people. I had always had a heart for youth and discovered that all they wanted was someone to listen, encourage, and empathize with them. However, this third quarter in our marriage after our children were out on their own afforded time to share in a similar capacity with young adult women, thus giving me a new mentoring field. I began to pray that I would never get too old to listen, care, and pray for those who needed me, which was one of my greatest joys in life. Besides working with the youth, Bernie began to have other mentoring opportunities of his own, first professionally and then with those who sought his personal advice. All this led to closer fellowship with some of our younger married friends. It became an enriching dimension in our marriage.

Snookie has developed numerous relationships with young and old. It has been interesting to observe what a wonderful friend she is to so many. It is not uncommon for her to receive an invitation to lunch or coffee with a postscript that says, "I need a little 'Snookie' time." I just smile because I know exactly what they mean.

We learned that having young friends helped keep us at least thinking young. Probably because of these relationships (and the longevity of our marriage), we began to be asked to lead marriage classes and share our experiences and ideas about how to have a strong Christian marriage. We were humbled by this honor and felt quite responsible for all we presented, so we drew not only from our own life together but also from research on the subject. We compiled a list of those things that add to as well as subtract from the success of a marriage. Our thoughts were intermingled with others to the point that we hardly knew what was originally ours. Suffice it to say, hardly anything is original anymore; it has just been repackaged. So here are some of the repackaged ideas that we shared in our marriage classes.

A complicated yet intriguing fact came to light right from the start: Men and women are different. Take attraction, for example. Men and women are generally drawn to one another in two ways, visually and verbally. By nature, men tend to be more visually oriented while women are more verbally oriented. Such things contribute to the mystique of marriage.

We are all creatures of habit and as such tend to follow repetitive patterns. This being the case, the question then becomes, what will enable us to embrace good habits and forsake bad ones? The failure to develop good habits is in itself a bad habit. This is true in life and particularly in the marriage relationship. Your habits as well as your mate's can often either enhance or inhibit this special partnership. Have you ever heard someone say, "That habit of his (hers) drives me crazy?" In this regard, here are a few suggestions that have helped us nurture our relationship:

Be intentional—good habits don't usually happen unless planned; bad ones often result from default.

Be diligent—good habits generally grow out of positive activity; bad ones can come from idleness.

Be disciplined—good habits are a matter of controlled effort; bad ones tend to be lawless.

Be a practitioner—good habits require practice; bad ones follow urges.

Be passionate—good habits build you up; bad ones let you down.

Be committed—good habits require a lot of effort; bad ones very little.

Be loving—good habits convey love; bad ones express disdain.

Our actions toward each other are generally driven by our habits. Give thought to how well you relate and interact with your spouse; often this is the direct result of your habits.

Someone sent us one of those Maxine cartoons where she bemoans, "Sure, marriage can be fun some of the time. Trouble is, you're married all of the time!" There's a bit of truth in that because once you get married, you are married all the time. But if you are married to your best friend, that should be a joyful thing. Add deep love, trust, and respect to that friendship, and you have the ingredients for a relationship like no other. However, the foundation, both individually and as a couple, must be faith in God in order to withstand the daily ups and downs. We are reminded often in the Bible that troubles will come, but He will be enough to not only carry us through but also to restore us to abundant life. His grace and mercies are new every morning!

So, you say, marriage sounds like a snap! Just be friends in love and ask the Lord to bless your marriage. Not so. Even a casual friendship requires something on your part. Did you know that almost all marriage problems are rooted in *self-centeredness*? The common causes of divorce—addictions of all kinds, including infidelity; financial burdens centered on wanton overspending; and leading separate lives with overcrowded schedules, to mention just a few—all fall into the category of self-centeredness. In fact, anything that you put ahead of your bond with your spouse other than your relationship with God raises a red flag!

I (Bernie) believe that being conscious of the needs of your spouse is one of the first steps to marital harmony and fulfillment. Of course, the next step is to act on it. Be proactive; seek ways to serve and care for your spouse. Even try to anticipate his or her desires. In my case, this means giving my best to Snookie in not only big things but also the small ones. Here is an example that you might think is trivial, but I don't. When I cut up strawberries for our breakfast, I search to find the best of the bunch for her plate. This was just the opposite of my attitude as a child. I always wanted the biggest and best for myself. And when I (Snookie) serve dinner, I always give Bernie the largest portions. That's even biblical! It reminds us to give of ourselves to meet the needs of our beloved. Marriage takes commitment, patience, understanding, forgiveness, kindness, and emotional and sexual fidelity. As one of our longtime ministers put it, love is not just a feeling; it's an action. Even in the little things.

As we shared with other couples in our classes and on retreats, we grew in our own understanding of just what we had committed to each other so long ago. This union is the real deal, and there are no substitutes. Sharing each other's lives *emotionally* means to open up to each other the deepest recesses of our hearts. Sharing *physically* means not only giving ourselves to each other sexually and lovingly but also working toward developing a healthy lifestyle of eating and exercise. It also involves making the most of what we have to work with appearance-wise. We should never take that for granted. Sharing *spiritually* means not only blending what we have learned from Bible study but also praying together regularly. All these things work together to create oneness in a marriage. We called this third quarter *Maturing Love* for a reason.

We were beginning to learn just how wonderful it is to be growing old together!

"I love you!"

"I know!"

Lessons Learned in the Third Quarter

1. Life's second half may require a change in direction and mind-set.
2. Experiencing deep personal loss and enduring difficult circumstances as partners can bring spouses closer; it is special to cry together.
3. Your spouse becomes more beautiful when viewed from God's perspective.
4. Even small expressions of love and affection are powerful.
5. Money can be a problem or a blessing.
6. Your reputation is one of your most prized possessions.
7. Having younger friends keeps you young.
8. Counseling and mentoring benefit the provider as much as the recipient.
9. Self centeredness is the root of most marital discord.
10. The third quarter is focused on *maturing love.*

Chapter 7

FOURTH QUARTER: LASTING LOVE

Many waters cannot quench love; rivers cannot wash it away.

—Song of Songs 8:7

How do you begin the fourth quarter? In football, a new tradition has begun in recent years. Players on each team hold up four fingers as a gesture of commitment for maximum effort to finish the game victoriously. Irrespective of the score at the end of the third quarter, the team members pledge to give it their all. It seems to us that a similar commitment is also appropriate in our game of life as husband and wife.

Grand Entry into Retirement

It was approximately two months before my (Bernie's) retirement, and I was already in the post-career mode. One of the projects on my list was to cut down a large dead pine tree in our side yard. It was among other trees, so I did the prudent thing and tied it to another tree to assure the correct trajectory of the fall into the woods. Guess I learned the hard way that dead trees are very unpredictable! The fall started in the right direction, but when it met resistance from the other trees, it broke off and began to come down the opposite way. I tried my best to escape and thankfully at least had the presence of mind to throw the chain saw to the side as I ran. But the bulk of the trunk hit me directly. After I felt the impact on my upper back and right shoulder, I lay on the ground for about twenty minutes, trying not to go into shock. It took me that long to muster the strength to get into the house. It's interesting what goes through your mind in such times of crisis. I remember thinking, *I am going to die just a couple of months before I retire. Snookie will probably remarry, and her next husband will enjoy the fruits of all my hard work and labor.* It sounds funny now, but it was very serious then.

Snookie, however, was my hero. She kept her cool, which helped me keep mine. She did not scold me for my poor judgment—that came later when she decreed prohibitions on some of my handyman activities. I was in the hospital overnight with a fractured scapula and cracked ribs. Both the ER physician and the orthopedist indicated quite frankly that if the tree had hit me just four inches to the left, I would be either dead or paralyzed. Fortunately, today I experience very few physical repercussions from all this, but what a way to begin the fourth quarter!

CEO of the Home

Bernie's official retirement as CEO of one of the largest health systems in the region began with a big reception honoring him. It was a gathering of members of our family as well as personal and professional friends from far and wide. It was a fitting tribute to a man who considered his work to be both his calling and his ministry. I was so honored to be by his side in that wonderful career and now looked forward to time we could spend together traveling, enjoying those grandchildren we had anticipated, and opening our homes in Marietta and in the North Carolina mountains to family and friends. Little did I know that my life in my own home would be undergoing a distinct change.

We laugh about it now, but all of a sudden, there were no quiet reading hours after lunch, little privacy to just try on and check out what I wanted to wear without an opinion, and few opportunities to catch up on the phone or computer without feeling like someone was waiting in line. Plus there was now a need to check in with somebody before I left the house. Didn't that somebody, who had been in charge of a huge corporation, know that I was CEO of the home? After I explained all that to him (ha), we settled into a give-and-take routine; not perfect, but workable. Bernie seemed happy to no longer be a CEO and even began to cherish the "honey do" tasks I delegated to him. We agreed on a division of labor since we both were now operating out of the same headquarters. For example, Bernie prepares breakfast every morning (wonderful to have it in bed), and I cook dinner in the evening. For lunch, we are on our own, although we sometime share a can of soup, fruit, or a sandwich.

Despite our best efforts to cooperate and coordinate, however, we still from time to time end up in a conflict. You may remember my reference to our children and their friends when they were together too long or in tight quarters, "two dogs in a pen." Bernie and I can do some growling and barking of our own but then can smile or laugh when we realize that we are acting like "two dogs in a pen!" Additionally, it has been important for each of us to have our own time apart, such as participating in different Bible studies and other church-related functions and volunteering in various community agencies, recreational activities, etc. fill this purpose.

After spending only a few months in the fourth quarter, something very significant occurred to me (Bernie). We both had been so busy up to this point in our marriage that we really had never spent this much quality time together. Although we had been married almost forty years, we were getting to know each other even better. And I really liked her! So one day, I just said, "Snookie, I need to share this with you. Since I'm home more now, I've really gotten to know you better. And I want you to know that I really like you!" I didn't think that this was such a big deal, but her reaction was that I had just given her the best present ever.

Grandchildren

Nowhere in the dictionary is there a good enough definition to describe grandchildren. Nor is there a description of what it means to be a grandparent that holds a candle to the great honor it truly is. We love our children unconditionally and that dimension has expanded to encompass their little ones. It's a love with a double whammy! Our experience actually began in the third quarter of our lives with the birth of Lindsey Elizabeth Dewhurst to our daughter Jenny and her husband, Bob. She was followed by Alexandria Elizabeth Brown, daughter of Jeff and Susan, and Jordan Bradley McLean, son of Amanda and Brad (born just before Pappy's retirement party). All lived in the Atlanta area at the time, so we anticipated watching them grow up close at hand. This was not to be, however. The Dewhursts were the first to go as they moved to Hickory, North Carolina, to establish a chair factory. Then Brad felt the call to go into the ministry, and they left for Louisville, Kentucky, to attend the Baptist seminary there. By then, Jeff and Susan had Noah Jeffrey, and the McLeans had Nathan Jesse to add to the Brown's grandchildren list. Now we had two more cities to visit as we made trips to be with our children and grandchildren. We wanted to be a part of their lives no matter how far away they were.

As it turned out, we got to know Louisville far better than we had planned. About a year or so after Greta Annette came into the McLean family, her brother

Nathan began experiencing some health problems. The end result was devastating to our close family. Nathan was diagnosed with a childhood cancer with a name that was totally foreign to us—neuroblastoma. The name had Stage Four preceding it, and that was the worst of the worst as far as we were concerned. Our little guy was only three years old, and he had surgery, chemotherapy, radiation, and two stem cell transplants ahead of him. It was too much to even grasp; we just thanked our heavenly Father for being there and went step-by-step through it all. God used modern medicine, the prayers of family and friends, and the faith of Nathan's devoted parents to bring him to where he is today, five years in remission. We are claiming healing for this precious boy who every day brings light to those around him.

A couple of years ago, we added two more grandchildren when Marc Bailey came into our lives. He and Jenny were married following her divorce, so his daughters Amanda and Brittany are now ours. They are all grown up in their twenties and are out on their own, but we are getting to know them through occasional visits. Amanda is in health care with an eye clinic, and Brittany is following her dream as a dancer in New York City.

We are blessed to be able to watch all these children grow. Lindsey is a good student with a winsome personality, bringing lots of friends her way. She is looking forward to college in just one more year. Alexandria is also a girl with high ideals for her education, is a cheerleader for her middle school, and is a genuinely sweet young lady. Jordan does well in school, plays tennis, and is in the middle school band. He is in the throes of adolescence and is "working on maturity" (his words). Some adults could take a lesson from him. Noah is interested in all things that are sports related. He is especially good at both basketball and baseball and practices hard to get it right. We enjoy watching his enthusiasm and teamwork. He's a winner! Nathan is full speed ahead with all he does regardless of some challenges that could hold him back. He will always make it happen with his charm and wit. Greta is the baby of the bunch but does a great job keeping up with the rest, even with two brothers giving her some grief. Her life is either way up or way down; one day she will be on stage with her pretty singing voice and her "dramatic training!" We are praying to be around to observe how they all turn out, knowing that it will be something special to see. Incidentally, they call us Grammy and Pappy.

Our Children Now

Of course, we would not have these wonderful grandchildren without our own children. As we write this, all three are now in their forties, happily married, and successful in their individual areas of activity. And most importantly, they are Christians and active in their local churches. Our oldest, Jenny, and her husband, Marc, live in Hickory, North Carolina. He is an executive with an aviation company that has developed a new corporate jet; Jenny is in the human resources department (her major field) with a large tape manufacturer. Jeff, our son, is a senior health care consultant (his major) with one of the largest consulting firms in the country; his wife, Susan, a former schoolteacher, is a stay-at-home mom who is constantly on the move with their two active children. Amanda, our youngest, and her husband, Brad, are deeply involved in ministry activities. He is the bi-vocational pastor at a small church and is also involved with an organization that provides contract administrative/financial services to other churches. Amanda works with him in both areas and, also a former teacher, substitute teaches at her children's elementary school. We are so proud of our children, their spouses, and, of course, our grandchildren. We realize that pride is not viewed positively in the Bible, but we believe that God will give us a pass with the kind of pride and love we have for all the members of our family.

Vacation Home

Earlier in our life story, I (Snookie) mentioned that we had made a providential visit to Lake Junaluska, North Carolina, with the choir from our church in Augusta. This is the Southeastern Jurisdiction Retreat Center for our United Methodist Church besides being a Smoky Mountain vacation home mecca. The choir director and his wife, who took us there, had become special friends, and this place was close to their hearts. We visited them later at the vacation home they ultimately bought there and began to see the value of having such a place for our own family, so we asked them to keep an eye out for us at Lake J.

God came calling once again and a planned dinner out with them in Atlanta became another weekend trip to their Lake J home. Right after we got there, we set out on a walk around the lake, and there it was—a big For Sale sign with a flyer in the box beside it. The price had been lowered and was now feasible for us. By the time that weekend was over, we had a new house with one of the best views on the lake. But the most telling evidence of God's hand in it all came much later when we were cleaning out some closets at my mother's house. She had kept a letter that I wrote her after our original trip to Lake J. In it, I had mentioned the beauty, serenity, and warmth of the surroundings, and that it would be a great place to have a vacation home one day.

We bought that home at the very beginning of our retirement years, anticipating the opportunity to use it not only for our family but also for what we consider our God-given hospitality ministry. In these past thirteen years, it has been used for vacations, retreats, family reunions, conferences, short sabbaticals, weekend getaways, times for refreshing and refueling for both family and friends (old and new), and even for a couple of honeymoons. Every time we cross the North Carolina line and see the Smokies looming in the distance, we experience calm and peace like none other. Lake J is our home away from home but without all the everyday "stuff" that commands our attention. We have been blessed immeasurably by this gift.

Our Mothers

As we are progressing through the fourth quarter, we find ourselves giving more and more thought to where we are now and how we got here. Who we are as individuals and ultimately as a couple is the result of relationships with many who have traveled with us along the way. If we were asked, "Who has had the greatest influence in making you who you are today?" we both would answer, "My mother!" We would like for you to meet them.

When I think of my (Snookie's) mother, I think of love first and then faith, strength, strong will, artistic talent, and all the qualities of a good friend. At age ninety-four, she has many friends of all ages. She was a wonderful example for me growing up because, even in times of adversity, she reassured me that I was loved and cared for. She showed me the face of what homemaking looked like, and I thought it to be a most noble profession. When my dad died at the age of fifty and she was left with three children at home, she examined her resources and did what she needed to do to supplement her income. Her art also helped fill her lonely hours without Daddy as she made a distinct contribution to her community. In time, I watched her make a new life with Howard in her second marriage. She is still making a difference in the lives of others by selling her paintings for charitable causes. She is a friend and mentor to those around her. I want to be just like her one day.

Mom was married when she was eighteen and had me (Bernie), her firstborn, when she was twenty. She died when she was ninety-three, so she and I had a relationship for seventy-three years. She was a special lady; she loved everyone, and everyone loved her. She was a person of deep faith. I have her last Bible and have benefited from her notes and markings in it. Hospitality was her strong suit, and her greatest joy was having guests in her home. My dad had a massive stroke when he was sixty-two, which meant that Mom became the leader at home when she was in her early fifties. She worked for almost twenty-five years as a housekeeping director at a church conference center. She wrote a children's book at age ninety that is being used throughout the state of Georgia to encourage reading and literacy among pre-K and kindergarten students. She had unusual strength and poise. I observed her crying only twice—once when my dad gave me a whipping and once when he died. She taught us all many lessons but mainly how to love unconditionally. I could not have had a better mom.

The Masterpiece

As I indicated earlier, my (Snookie's) mother is an artist, so I know all about blank canvases sitting around waiting to be brought to life. I think a Christ-centered marriage begins that same way. It's a work of art in the making, put together by two imperfect but forgiven people with the guidance of a perfect God. But, you say, life can throw some really hard stuff at you, creating swirls of agony on that canvas! Maybe our road has been less rocky than some, depending on how you look at it, but I think those are the times we have added character to our canvas. Bernie and I have found that those harsh lines on our artwork soften when we quit trying to handle circumstances around us on our own and give them over to our God who is in this marriage with us. Here in the fourth quarter, we have come to realize that He is the only One who can ensure that we end up with the masterpiece He wants us to have.

"I love you more than ever!"

"Me too!"

Lessons Learned in the Fourth Quarter

1. Having purpose in the fourth quarter is just as important as it is in the first three.
2. After retirement, the roles of marriage partners will change.
3. More available time and freedom provides great opportunities to grow as a couple in areas that may have been neglected.
4. Grandchildren truly are the reward for having children.
5. Prayer makes a difference.
6. A vacation home can be a means of expanding the ministry of hospitality.

7. Emulating those individuals who had a positive influence on you is an excellent way to become a good role model for others.

8. Our blended lives are much like an artist's canvas that is evolving into a painting—hopefully, a masterpiece.

9. The fourth quarter of life in the context of marriage may be classified as *lasting love.*

Chapter 8

POETRY: EXPRESSIONS OF LOVE AND FAITH

We both enjoy writing. It is a way to express some of our deepest feelings and beliefs. At times, these efforts are through journal entries, a note to a friend, recording a thought in the margin of our Bibles, or composing an article and even a book. Our writings take many forms, but one of the most rewarding is poetry. Here are a few of our attempts to share ourselves through verses that rhyme.

College Girl

Can it be, this lovely girl you see,
Can she really belong to me?
A college freshman with many dreams,
Oh, how incredibly grown-up she seems!

It wasn't easy to let her go,
And deep inside I still miss her so;
Those heart-to-heart talks, the smiles, the tears
As mother and daughter we've shared through the years.

What happened to time? It seemed to fly
From long blond ponytails skating by
*To dances, **the** car, guys in the den,*
What a pleasure, a real joy it has been!

I cannot be sad; it's as it should be.
Her childhood is over, her wings soar free.
This is the beginning, part of the plan
That God holds for her in the palm of His hand.

(Written by Snookie when daughter
Jenny left for college)

Gone to Camp

The milkshake churn is silent,
The cookie jar is full.
The stairs are resting quietly,
In the hall there is a lull.
The ball has stopped it bouncing
And the screen door is intact.
The grass is growing steadily
In the front and in the back.
The washing machine load is lighter
And the grocery bill is down,
For the car there is no chauffeur
Waiting to drive us into town.
The twin beds are still made,
And the bedroom looks so neat.
The rug is in its place,
Undisturbed by scuffling feet.
What is missing here? you ask.
There seems to be an empty gap!
It's the absence of a boy of fifteen
Who has simply gone to camp.

(Written by Snookie for son Jeff when at camp)

The Handprints Are Higher This Year

Little handprints on the wall
Reaching higher; toward the Fall.
Can it be she's six this year
With the dawn of school so near?
It seems but a day since life began,
First she crawled, and then she ran.
The youngest of three; a joy to behold,
Who is this sprite that's grown so bold?
Let her go? Oh yes, we must.
She has more to learn than can be taught by us.
For it's not only the "3Rs" that matter,
But also a lesson called "working together."
She and her classmates will study, laugh, and play;
Do all sorts of projects, during the course of a day.
Then when afternoon comes and the bell has rung,
We'll share with her all she's done.
She can't wait—It's we who hesitate.

(Written by Snookie for daughter
Amanda starting school)

Bridging the Gap

There is a gap 'tween God and me.
Must bridge that gap so I can be
Someone who finds that long-lost key.
Please, God, come down and set me free.
I live a life that's all 'bout me;
The world says take, and I agree.
Fortune and fame are what I seek,
Yet peace and joy I cannot keep.
Refrain
The Word came down, said, "Follow me";
I did just that, now I can see.
He gave His life on a rugged tree;
I met Him there at Calvary.
We bridged that gap 'tween God and me;
And praise to Him, I now can be
One who has found that long-lost key.
He rose again and set me free!
Refrain
Oh, Oh! Bridging the gap is a lifetime goal;
Bridging the gap can make me whole;
Bridging the gap whether young or old;
Bridging the gap to save my soul.

(Written by Snookie and Bernie as a
poem and then later put to music)

A Time to Run

There is a time when you've yet to run;
And you feel that day will never come.
You crawl, then walk, and at last you run;
The race of life has just begun!

There is a time when you enjoy the run;
And you sense your turn has finally come.
You leap at the sound of the starting gun;
The race begun seems easily won.

There is a time when you only run;
And you wonder what you have become.
Days lack meaning at every turn;
This race through life is far less fun!

There is a time when you cannot run,
And you fear that your days will flee;
Then you hear, "Though you cannot run,
You can walk or just talk with Me."
There is a time when you cease to run
Or walk or talk or see;
Then the gates open and you'll hear, "Well done.
Now run, my child, run to Me."

(Composed by Bernie in appreciation
to the generation who raised him)

My Prayer

Lord,
We know so little
Yet want so much of what this world has to offer.
Help us to know more
So we'll want less of the world and more of You!
Amen

(Written by Bernie at a time of introspection)

Chapter 9

REFLECTIONS AND CONCLUSIONS

We both have read this manuscript numerous times to catch any errors and to make it more readable and understandable. Just as we prepared to submit it for editing, it hit us that maybe our story *is* somewhat of a fairy tale or as a good friend remarked, "You two have lived a charmed life." We would disagree with the latter since we have faced some significant challenges and obstacles (deaths, illnesses, relational and job issues, etc.). However, we have had a wonderful, fun-filled, satisfying life together, and it is true that we have been blessed beyond measure. Are we normal and typical or is our story an exception in today's world? We honestly don't know. But we have learned a few things in our fifty years together that we feel are worth passing along and thus bear repeating.

First, we believe that our story, as well as that of other couples, comfortably fits into the "four quarter game" template that we chose to use. This has made it much easier for us to review and analyze our marriage and its progression. Our collaborative effort to record our story has been an unbelievable experience that has afforded us the opportunity to look back, reminisce, marvel, understand, and appreciate each other more than ever. We have laughed and cried, we have remembered things that should never be forgotten, and we have regained some of the lost twinkle as we look into each other's eyes. We have fallen in love all over again. We recommend that all married couples go through a similar exercise (be sure to exclude certain experiences that might be hurtful and painful that have no redeeming qualities). Using the "four quarter" template, relive and record your story for yourselves, your children, and others. You, too, will be blessed!

Second, we believe that even though marriage is a serious and solemn covenant, it also should be full of joy, fun, and excitement. It should not be burdensome to share your lives together. Instead, this relationship should be a constantly growing process of appreciating each other and truly becoming one. In addition to the joy of physical intimacy, it should foster emotional and spiritual closeness. Sharing the good and bad of each other's day, taking a walk-and-talk time, watching television together, having a date night without children, working together on a redecorating project, or making plans for the next day are just a few of the little things that promotes heartfelt oneness. In addition to *loving* your spouse, you should also *like* him or her. Enjoy each other!

Third, marriage is all about family. In our case, as the two of us became one and started our family, we also, in a true sense, joined our two original ones together. In an instant, we each had an additional mother and father and brothers and sisters (in-laws). Some of these new relationships have been closer than others, but they all have resulted in an expansion of family. Then, when our children came along, our family of two ultimately became five (and later even larger with their spouses and children). All this means that there are more folks to love. Thankfully, when our children and grandchildren arrived, we discovered that we did not need to divide the same amount of love among more; instead, God has given us unlimited capacity in this regard. Our love for each other has actually grown along with our family.

And, finally, we believe that there is a God who has a plan for us individually and collectively, and that His plan is better than any we might independently develop on our own. It includes instructions for our relationship as husband and wife that, if followed, will result in a blessed marriage. We have a choice to totally or partially accept or reject God's plan for us. Unfortunately, we often knowingly or unknowingly reject it, resulting in something less than what God has in mind for us. Additionally, we live in a fallen world that often allows bad things to happen to good people, and we all will experience times of pain and suffering. We believe that marriage is a trinity relationship between a husband and wife with an almighty God. For it to be effective, there must be agreement and commitment by all three parties. The problem occurs when either the husband or wife break the agreement or fail to honor the commitment. The Lord has never broken His promises! Marriage is a holy and sacred relationship that should not be entered into without understanding its true cost, benefit, and purpose.

We are still very much alive and "God ain't through with us yet." We don't know what the future holds, but we do know who holds the future. So we arise every day anticipating what He has in store for us. As we end our story, our prayer is that through our thoughts, words, and deeds we bring honor and glory to Him.

In our final reviews, we both noticed that one particular word has been used over and over in our story. We even made an effort to reduce its use somewhat. But no matter how hard we have tried, we have not found a better term to truly convey the message that we want to share. So we will close by using it one more time. "We have been *blessed*!"

EPILOGUE

Our Prayer

We felt that we should include an additional thought that may possibly be the most vital one we share. An important and effective way that we can foster a Christ-centered marriage and home is to pray together regularly. Thankfully, we learned this relatively early and routinely start each day with this special time with the Lord. We take turns praying. Interestingly, we have developed a pattern that we follow that guides our minds and hearts. Certainly, we deviate from this when something weighs heavily on us, but we have found that there is nothing wrong with structured and organized prayer. Actually, Jesus gave us one in the Lord's Prayer. The important thing is that we are truly engaged with our God who is such an integral part of our marriage. It will vary each day in length and specifics, and at times, it becomes a three-way conversation. Here is our model prayer:

Dear Lord,

(Praise) We are so blessed to have You as our heavenly Father, Master, and Savior. We praise, worship, and love You.

(Thanksgiving) Thank You for a new day and for Your many blessings and provisions and for life itself.

(Intercession) We specifically lift up and pray for our family (immediate and extended), our friends, our church (pastors), country (president and other leaders), the world (peace and justice), and particularly those in need (physically, emotionally, and especially spiritually).

(Forgiveness) And, Lord, we pray for ourselves—we fall so short. Please forgive us for our sins of commission and particularly omission.

(Petition/Guidance) We are currently involved in writing a book about our marriage. Please guide us in this effort, and use it in any way that's pleasing to You, even if it's just for ourselves.

(Special thanks) And thank You, Lord, for being such an important part of our marriage. And thank You for my honey, lover, and best friend and for the wonderful relationship we have. She/he is not only special to me but also to our children, grandchildren, family, and friends. You have blessed me with the most wonderful life partner. Give him/her a great day!

(Recognition) We realize that we are Yours. Please indwell us with Your Holy Spirit, and use us this day to

further Your kingdom. And we pray that all we do will bring honor and glory to You.

We humbly pray in the blessed name of Your Son and our Savior, Jesus Christ!

Amen

YOUR STORY

You probably noticed that we have suggested several times that you as a couple record your own story. Please remember that every life is unique, resulting in a somewhat different game plan for each; therefore, your story will be an original drama. Many factors can play a part; death, illness, divorce, economics, personal revelations, and other happenings can change the course of your history. This doesn't mean our story is better than yours or, conversely, that your way is right and ours is wrong, but rather that our lives have just taken different paths. The circumstances in which we find ourselves are far less important than our responses to them.

In addition to sharing something very special with your children and/or those who come after you, this exercise will do wonders for your own relationship with each other. Certainly, you must approach this both positively and sensitively. We all have parts of our lives that we do not want to rehash. Focus on those experiences and stories that uplift and affirm your mate and/or from which you learned valuable lessons. To this end, we offer the following journal format for your use. Its purpose is to assist you when and if you decide to begin writing your story. To use this, it will be important that you define your quarters as you see them, when they begin and when they end.

One additional thought: If you are reading this at the beginning of your marital journey, why not get a head start on writing your story by recording important events, times of personal and spiritual growth, etc. as you go along? Keeping a daily journal, as I (Snookie) have through the years is a most useful tool in this regard.

_____ and _____ Are Sweethearts
(*your names*)

Introduction

Define marriage and what it means to you as a couple. Is it turning out like you expected?

First Quarter: Awakening Love

Define awakening love. Describe your growing-up years. What do you think was preparing you to one day become someone's spouse? If you met at this point, describe the when and how.

Second Quarter: Growing Love

Define growing love. Was yours deepening? When did Christ become a part of your relationship? Share your work history. If you have children, record the experiences of parenthood.

Midlife: Crisis or Commitment

Define midlife. Did you experience crisis in any area? Was the empty nest a difficult adjustment? Did you look back with regret or look forward with anticipation?

Third Quarter: Maturing Love

Define maturing love. How did you prepare for and move into this new phase? Did you nurture your marriage as you had more time together, seeking to keep romance and excitement alive?

Fourth Quarter: Lasting Love

Define lasting love. Have health and wealth issues become more of a factor? Do you feel that God still has a purpose for your lives as individuals as well as a couple?

Reflections and Conclusions

(Express your love for each other, and share your hearts!)

ENDNOTES

[i] Cannon, Hughie. "Frankie and Johnny," Ballad, 1904.

[ii] Brown, Bernie. "Purpose in the Fourth Quarter," 2012, p. 78.

[iii] "Ritual, The Methodist Church." The Methodist Publishing House, 1956, p. 46.

[iv] "The Message." Copyright 1913, 1994, 1995, 1996, 2000, 2001, 2002 by NavPress Publishing Group, p. 4.

Front cover photograph by Lindsey Dewhurst, Snookie and Bernie's granddaughter

Bernie Brown is also the author of
LESSONS LEARNED ON THE WAY DOWN
A Perspective on Christian Leadership in a Secular World
And
PURPOSE IN THE FOURTH QUARTER
Finishing the Game of Life Victoriously
Visit www.purposeinthefourthquarter.com
Bernie's E-mail address: bernielb@bellsouth.net
Snookie's E-mail address: snookierb@bellsouth.net